PRAISE FOR *DE*

Heather Dixon inhales and exhales Jesus! Even .... hard, she is determined to make every day of her life count for eternity. In her study *Determined*, powerful Bible teaching meets encouraging practical application, giving you the opportunity to soak and study through large chunks of Scripture as well as thoughtful personal questions that challenge and nurture new insights. If you long to follow Jesus' example of determined living, this study will encourage and equip you along the way.
—**Barb Roose**, speaker and author of *Joshua: Winning the Worry Battle* and *Winning the Worry Battle: Life Lessons from the Book of Joshua*

The abundant life isn't a distant dream but a reality for every believer who follows Jesus' example. What we should determine most is that what was true for Jesus is true for us. Thankfully, Heather specifies the footsteps we can follow.
—**Micca Campbell**, author of *An Untroubled Heart: Finding a Faith Stronger Than All Your Fear*

We live in an era where it's easier to give up and tune out than to stay the course and determine our hearts and minds to be the change this world needs. In *Determined*, Heather challenges us to leave apathy behind and dive deeper into an unwavering, joy-filled faith—a faith that mirrors the faith of our Savior, Jesus Christ. If you are ready to embrace life to the fullest while making an impact for the Kingdom, this study is for you!
—**Lauren Gaskill**, speaker and author of *Into the Deep: Diving into a Life of Courageous Faith*

This study is practical as well as insightful. Learning the aspects of a determined life such as Jesus exemplified is worth our time and attention, offering us the opportunity to realize the hope of living more like Jesus every day.
—**Gretchen Fleming**, author of *Press On: Encouragement to Keep You Moving When You Feel Overwhelmed*

Determined is an edifying and sound Bible study for those of us looking to make our precious minutes with God and others count. This study of the Gospel of Luke shows us how to let go of burdens so we can live with more freedom, intention, and abundance. Heather helps us determine how to be completely committed to Jesus, inspiring us to live lives of purpose and praise just as Jesus did.
—**Tracy Steel**, speaker and author of *A Redesigned Life: Uncovering God's Purpose When Life Doesn't Go as Planned*

Determined will help you make a big impact in God's kingdom! Heather is a dynamite speaker and equally powerful author. Whether your life is turbulent or smooth sailing, this study of Luke will show you how to be guided by Jesus through your day-to-day journey.
—**Sarah Philpott**, author of *Loved Baby: 31 Devotions to Helping You Grieve and Cherish Your Child After Pregnancy Loss*

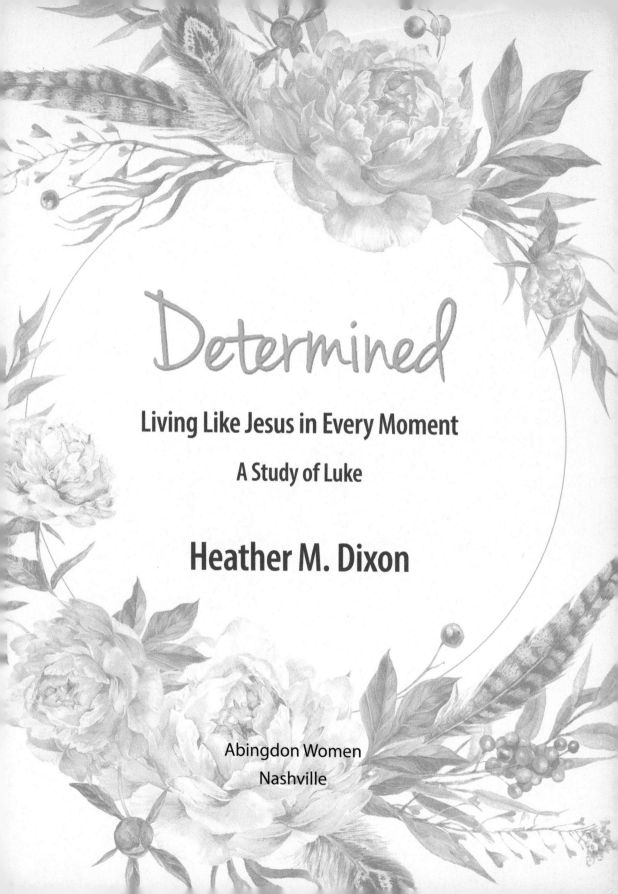

Determined

Living Like Jesus in Every Moment

A Study of Luke

Heather M. Dixon

Abingdon Women
Nashville

Determined
Living Like Jesus in Every Moment

ISBN 978-1-5018-7886-2

19 20 21 22 23 24 25 26 27 28 — 10 9 8 7 6 5 4 3
MANUFACTURED IN THE UNITED STATES OF AMERICA

Contents

About the Author

Heather M. Dixon is an author, speaker, and Bible teacher who understands living with a story that is not easy. Diagnosed with an incurable and terminal genetic disorder that she inherited from her mother, she is passionate about encouraging and equipping women to trust in God, face their greatest fears, and live with hope, especially in the midst of difficult circumstances. When she is not blogging at The Rescued Letters or speaking at women's conferences and events, Heather loves to make the most of everyday moments such as cooking for her husband and son, brainstorming all the possible ways to organize Legos and superheroes, checking out way too many library books, or unashamedly indulging in her love for all things Disney. Heather is the author of *Determined: Living Like Jesus in Every Moment*, *Ready: Finding the Courage to Face the Unknown* and a regular contributor to *Journey* magazine.

Follow Heather:

🐦 @rescuedletters

📷 @rescuedletters

f @rescuedletters

📌 @rescuedletters

Her blog: therescuedletters.com
(check here also for event dates and booking information)

Introduction

For most of us, life is busy. On some days simply accomplishing the tasks set before you can seem like the hardest of feats. In the midst of all the usual busyness, there are inconveniences such as last-minute errands, family obligations, or perhaps a new puppy that won't stop chewing your furniture. Then there are the heavier things: a family member is walking through something you're not equipped to handle, you have to process the death of a loved one, your health falters under stress, or there's a sudden but all-encompassing change that throws the routines you've come to depend on into disarray. Life is full of distractions, pulling us in every way but God's way. And sometimes the most challenging thing we have to do is simply stay the course.

It's easy to wander through life without appreciating the gift of every moment we've been given. When we're driven by distraction, we overlook the rich rewards of walking hand in hand with Jesus. The result? An unsatisfying life, missed opportunities to experience the joy of being in sync with God, and days marked with apathy and anxiety instead of passion and peace. Our time on earth is measured. We should want to make *every* moment count—not only because we aren't guaranteed the next one—but also because this is exactly how our Savior spent His time here.

How, then, do we walk out unwavering and joy-filled faith every day, determined to let go of the things that keep us from experiencing abundant life and fulfilling the plans God has for us? The answers are found in following the footsteps of the One who lived fully, because He was determined that we might do the same.

As I wrote this study, Jesus gave me a master class in determined living, because I had to fight to stay focused and finish in the midst of all the distractions of life—many of them good things. I wrote in my office surrounded by books and in my kitchen with my goldendoodle biting my toes; in a hockey rink during my son's practice and in the car as my husband was driving us three hundred miles down the road; on an ironing board in a closet on vacation and on the back porch with the breeze blowing my papers away; in the carpool line, on the couch, at the coffeehouse, and in between sessions at a conference. Even now I'm writing this introduction from the parking lot of a fast-food restaurant in the middle of a fierce storm.

But through it all Jesus taught me what we are about to study together, and it begins with this: the first step to living with determination is laying *everything* at Jesus' feet. Whatever you are bringing into this study, Jesus is ready to pick it up; so let's agree to start there. Take a moment now to release the worries of your heart to Him before you read any further. We'll only be as determined as we are willing to trust our Teacher.

My prayer is that through our time together Jesus will reveal to you that the burdens you carry do not determine your capacity for contentment or your ability to make a kingdom impact for Christ. Only by learning from His example will you determine to live like Him in spite of what life throws your way. If the burdens you carry ever pose a threat to your peace, you're in the right place. We're not going to learn how to *live with* them; we're going to learn how to *live abundantly through* them.

In this six-week study of Luke, we will follow the life and ministry of Jesus as we consider the choices He made on His way to the cross. We'll intimately connect with a Savior who remained laser-focused on His mission to love the world. In return, we'll receive a model for intentional living that we can replicate to ensure we are living each day to the fullest and making a difference for God's kingdom. And together we'll determine to embrace the abundant life we are promised in Jesus.

It's time to stop wandering and start living!

Getting Started

As we dive into the Gospel of Luke, we will be equipped for determined living, learning to emulate Jesus every day. Here's what you'll find within these pages:

- **Five days of lessons for every week of study.** If we want to hear from God, we've got to be in His Word. There isn't an easy way around this. To get the most out of this study, this is where you'll want to spend the bulk of your time. Each day's lesson will guide you through personal study of a passage from Luke as well as application of what you've learned.
- **Extra Insights.** These are additional thoughts and comments in the margin to help you dive deeper into the cultural context or theological topic for a particular passage.
- **A suggested Reading Plan for the entire Gospel of Luke.** To stay focused on our scope of determined living, we won't study every passage in the Gospel of Luke in detail. But the reading plan provides an option for a full survey of Luke's Gospel. (Watch for the notes in the margin.)
- **A Video Viewer Guide for each group session.** Although you can do this study individually and reap benefits, it is designed to be done with a group for encouragement, support, and accountability. The weekly video teaching compliments all that you have studied on your own throughout the week. You can use the Video Viewer Guide at the end of each week's lessons to follow along and jot down any additional notes from the video teaching.

I recognize that certain stages of life allow for certain levels of participation. I've had times in my own life when finding just five spare minutes for Bible study presented a challenge as well as quieter seasons of life that allowed for leisurely time in God's Word. I understand different times call for different commitments. So I have designed this study to meet you where you are. With God's guidance, only you can determine the level of participation that suits your season of life. Remember to strive for the maximum amount of time in God's Word that you can with the least amount of anxiety. And remember: what works for your Bible study sisters may not work for you. Whatever you decide, I hope you'll find that the more you study His Word, the deeper you'll connect with Jesus.

Here are the levels of participation:

LEVEL 1:   Read the content from the weekly lessons and participate in the group sessions.

LEVEL 2:   Read the content from the weekly lessons, answer the questions, and participate in the group sessions.

LEVEL 3:   Read the content from the weekly lessons, answer the questions, complete the reading plan for each week, and participate in the group sessions.

After prayerfully considering your season of life and how God is leading you in this study, which level of participation seems to be the best fit for you? Circle it below:

1   2   3

One final word: determined living doesn't happen overnight, and it doesn't happen without the study of God's Word and the help of the Holy Spirit. If you will be in the Word, be faithful in prayer, and be bold in asking for the Spirit to move in you, I guarantee you that He will!

Much Love,

Heather

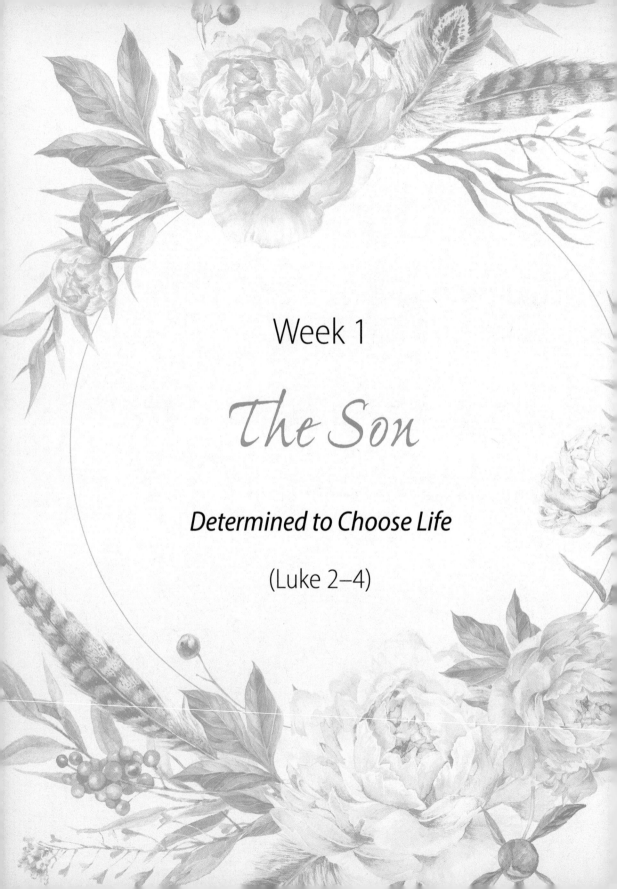

Week 1

The Son

Determined to Choose Life

(Luke 2–4)

> **Therefore be imitators of God, as beloved children.**
> **(Ephesians 5:1 ESV)**

I have not always been an early riser. I have clear memories of waking to the constant shrill of my alarm clock, fingers scrambling to find the button that would halt the noisy interrupter so I could continue my lazy morning dreams. Youth is blissfully ignorant of to-do lists and adult responsibilities, so I often indulged in the luxury of sleeping in when I was younger.

But family and jobs and laundry have a way of pulling us out of bed, do they not? There are people to love and work to do, and lazy morning dreams won't help us accomplish either. And so, my habit of sipping an early morning cup of coffee began out of necessity—with whipped cream, of course, and always before anyone else in the house was up.

As youth faded away, a steady routine began to form: stumble out of bed before the sunrise, press start on the miraculous coffee machine, brush teeth, pour coffee, and make my way to the back porch with my Bible in hand. I never wanted to get out of bed so early; but I knew that if I didn't, the rest of my day would feel unsettled. I needed the focus of my morning habit to set the intention for my day.

But what started as a necessity turned into a blessing. The quiet morning when no one else was awake gave way to peacefulness in my heart. The beauty of the sunrise, each one unique and never the same, was a faithful reminder of God's glory and provision. The sweet birdsongs as they greeted the new day became my own private symphony. And the memories I've collected spending one-on-one time with Jesus in those wee morning hours are some of the most precious that I know.

I don't know if you are an early riser or not. The answer doesn't matter much to the goal for our study. What does matter is our willingness to develop a habit of showing up. You and I are committing to six weeks of intimately connecting with a Savior who was determined to love us. What does He ask of us in return?

Show up.

Early morning? Lunch break? Right before bedtime? Pick the time that works for you and show up to meet Him in the pages of Luke. Some days it will feel like a necessity. Some days it will feel like a luxury. But I can guarantee you that pursuing a habit of meeting with Jesus will become one of your richest blessings.

In this inaugural week of our study, we're about to find that we are not the first to develop habits for success. Jesus is going to pave the way for us by His example, and I can't wait to dive into this first week with you. I am praying for your time in the Word, that in every moment you show up to meet with Jesus, He would nourish your heart with truth and wisdom.

DAY 1: WITNESS TO WORSHIP

Throughout our study we will be following in the footsteps of Jesus as we examine the choices He made on His way to the cross. Every day when we meet here together, we'll consider His words and actions—what He did and sometimes what He didn't do. Along the way, we'll apply His example for determined living so that we might emulate it and find the abundant life He has promised. For each day of our homework, we will focus our study solely on the miraculous life of Jesus. Except today.

The baby Jesus is just eight days old when we meet Him in the second chapter of Luke, and He certainly has something to teach us here. But there is someone else I'd like to introduce you to as we embark on our path toward determined living—someone we will meet in the Court of Women outside the Temple. I think you'll understand in a moment why we are starting with this woman. This week we are developing habits for success toward determined living, and today's heroine—or rather, today's witness—displays a habit that will be critical to our mission.

Read Luke 2:21-39, and put a placeholder there for future reference.

There are a lot of moving pieces, parts, and people in the Gospel of Luke. To help solidify them in our minds, we'll begin each day by briefly summarizing what we have just read before we dig deeper. This will get us into the habit of looking for narrative details as we read, paying attention to setting and character information as well. We'll call this section The Quick Three, and you'll see it just below the reading assignment for each day.

The Quick Three
What happened?
Where did it happen?
What characters are mentioned in this reading?

Determined living. It's what we are after in these six weeks together. Here's something you probably already know: determined living won't happen by accident. It will take a focused and intentional heart to move past the things that hinder us from living like Jesus. But by the end of our study together, we'll find that determined living is easier than we might think. The first step is always the hardest, and you've done that by opening this study. You're already on your way.

> Take a moment now to jot down a few examples from your life of things that have kept or might be keeping you from determined living. You might also want to add a description of what determined living means to you today. There isn't a right or wrong answer here. We're just opening our hearts to set the tone for our time together.

Setting the Scene

Now, let's set the scene for today as we see Jesus in His infancy, and then we'll settle in with what our heroine witness has to teach us. When we meet the Holy Family in this second chapter of Luke, we find them participating in two traditional Jewish ceremonies.

> Read Genesis 17:12. What does this verse tell us about the first of these ceremonies?

> What additional information about the child are we told in Luke 2:21?

After Jesus' circumcision, the family would travel to Jerusalem for the second ceremony because this ceremony had to take place in the Temple.

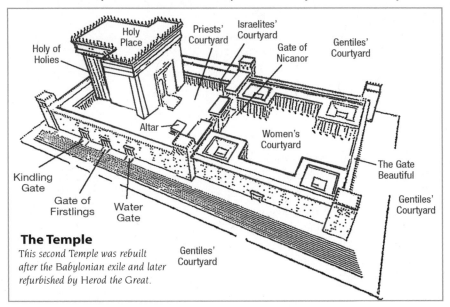

Holy of Holies · Holy Place · Priests' Courtyard · Israelites' Courtyard · Gate of Nicanor · Gentiles' Courtyard · Altar · Women's Courtyard · The Gate Beautiful · Gentiles' Courtyard · Kindling Gate · Gate of Firstlings · Water Gate · Gentiles' Courtyard

The Temple
This second Temple was rebuilt after the Babylonian exile and later refurbished by Herod the Great.

"Consecrate to me every firstborn male. The first offspring of every womb among the Israelites belongs to me, whether human or animal."

(Exodus 13:2)

Read Exodus 13:2 in the margin. What does it reveal about what is unfolding in this ceremony in the Temple?

These two ceremonies represented long-standing Jewish observances that were set in place centuries before Jesus was born. Why do you think it was important for Jesus' parents to fulfill these traditional rituals after His birth?

The Savior of the world had finally come, yet He would still have to abide by the sacred habits established by His heavenly Father. From the start of His life on earth, Jesus set the precedent that divine rules still applied, even for the one true King. There were no exemptions. There were no hallway passes out of what God had ordained as necessary and required for His people. As Warren Wiersbe explains, Jesus would obey His Father's wishes "perfectly."[3] And so, a circumcision was in order, along with a dedication ceremony where He would be set apart for God. Then we find Jesus and His family in the Court of Women, just outside the Holy of Holies in the Temple of the Lord (see the Temple diagram).

The scene that Mary and Joseph would have observed in the Court of Women would be similar to what is portrayed in Acts 2:46a and 3:1-2. Read this passage in the margin on page 15 and describe the activity in your own words:

Write the name of the gate mentioned in verse 2 here:

It was through the Beautiful Gate that the Jewish people would enter the Court of Women. The reason? As we just read in Acts 2:46, they were coming to the Temple to worship God. A rather aptly named gate, is it not? We are our most beautiful when our faces are turned toward the heavens in praise of who God is and all that He has done for us.

It's not easy to concisely define what worship means to me personally. So complex is the act of praising our Creator that even the original biblical languages of Hebrew, Aramaic, and Greek employ many different words to describe it.

Extra Insight

Mary and Joseph's sacrifice at the Temple fulfilled the requirements of a mother's purification after childbirth and a firstborn male's dedication to the Lord (Leviticus 12:1-8, Exodus 13:1-13). They were likely too poor to afford the standard offering of a lamb, so they brought the two turtledoves or pigeons deemed acceptable as a substitute. All the while, they have brought the Lamb Himself, who would become the sacrificial offering for sins of the entire world! (1 Peter 1:18-19).[2]

Read these verses that express God's vision for our worship, and put a check mark beside the ones that resonate most strongly with you today.

Sing to the Lord, for he has done glorious things;
    let this be known to all the world.
                                    (Isaiah 12:5)

Ascribe to the Lord the glory due his name;
    worship the Lord in the splendor of his holiness.
                                    (Psalm 29:2)

⁶Come, let us bow down in worship,
    let us kneel before the Lord our Maker;
⁷for he is our God
    and we are the people of his pasture,
    the flock under his care.
                                    (Psalm 95:6-7a)

Therefore, I urge you, brothers and sisters, in view of God's mercy, to offer your bodies as a living sacrifice, holy and pleasing to God—this is your true and proper worship.
                                    (Romans 12:1)

¹⁵Let the peace of Christ rule in your hearts, since as members of one body you were called to peace. And be thankful. ¹⁶Let the message of Christ dwell among you richly as you teach and admonish one another with all wisdom through psalms, hymns, and songs from the Spirit, singing to God with gratitude in your hearts. ¹⁷And whatever you do, whether in word or deed, do it all in the name of the Lord Jesus, giving thanks to God the Father through him.
                                    (Colossians 3:15-17)

Feel free to jot your favorite verse on worship in the margin if it's not listed above. Based on this selection of verses, how would you define God's vision for worship?

Do you have a habit of worship? If so, describe it here. If not, consider what a habit of worship might look like based on the verses above.

⁴⁶They worshiped together at the Temple each day . . .

³¹Peter and John went to the Temple one afternoon to take part in the three o'clock prayer service. ²As they approached the Temple, a man lame from birth was being carried in. Each day he was put beside the Temple gate, the one called the Beautiful Gate, so he could beg from the people going into the Temple.
(Acts 2:46a; 3:1-2 NLT)

How have you seen the act of worship positively change your life? If you can't think of any examples, how might a consistent habit of worship impact your day-to-day attitude?

And There Was a Prophetess

Our heroine for today knew the value of worship. In fact, she determined to dedicate her life's work to praising God. It's time that we meet her. Other than Mary, Joseph, and the baby Jesus, there are two additional characters mentioned in our reading for today.

Write their names here (see Luke 2:25, 36):

_____   _____

One witness is not enough to convict anyone accused of any crime or offense they may have committed. A matter must be established by the testimony of two or three witnesses.

(Deuteronomy 19:15 NIV)

As one scholar notes, Luke often places both a male and female character in specific situations in his writings to serve as dual witnesses.[4] Deuteronomy 19:15 might explain the reasoning behind this: two witnesses helped validate a testimony (see margin). The voices of Simeon and Anna together help to validate the birth of the Savior in a time when not everyone would readily recognize Him.

It's Anna's voice that I want us to hear. Although Luke doesn't record her actual words, her actions are more than enough to boldly proclaim the message that is on her heart.

Based on Luke 2:36-38, what do we know about Anna?

About how old was she?

Was she married?

How does Luke describe her occupation?

I really adore the way Luke introduces Anna's story in the New American Standard Bible translation: "And there was a prophetess, Anna the daughter of Phanuel, of the tribe of Asher" (Luke 2:36a). *And there was a prophetess.* Anna was no ordinary worshiper. She was God's spokesperson. A prophetess was simply a female prophet, one who "had a special gift of declaring and interpreting God's message."[5]

As a widowed woman in first-century Jerusalem, Anna didn't find herself daily praising God in the Court of Women by accident. In fact, societal trends of that time reveal that she was likely a minority in her decision to abandon all that she knew and commit the rest of her life to the Lord. The Apostle Paul gives us a glimpse of what would have been expected of widows.

Read 1 Timothy 5:3-16. Based on what verse 14 says, what would Anna have been strongly encouraged to do after her husband died?

We don't know what prompted Anna to make her home at the Temple after the death of her husband, but we can tell from her actions that she professed a deep devotion to her Lord.

Turn again to Luke 2:36-38 and answer the following questions:

How did Anna spend her days at the Temple?

Did she recognize Jesus as the Savior of the world, or did she treat Him as just an adorable baby in the courtyard?

Why do you think she recognized His identity so easily?

What was her response to seeing the baby Jesus?

We can tell from Anna's story that she was determined to worship her King against all odds. Societal customs for widowed women could not keep her from devoting her life to God. Because worshiping God was a priority for Anna, she is an example of a believer we want to emulate. And that's why we are beginning our journey to determined living with her: she was a witness who was determined to worship.

Can you recall a time when the choice to worship God conflicted with what was expected of you? If so, how did you respond?

Extra Insight

There are other prophetesses mentioned in the Bible. You can find them in Exodus 15:20; Judges 4:4; 2 Kings 22:14; Isaiah 8:1-4; and Acts 21:9.

And There Was a Woman Determined to Worship God

A worshipful heart prepares us for what we may meet in the coming day.

I asked you earlier how the act of worship has positively changed your life. For me, I am never more starkly aware of worship's value than when it is absent from my daily habits. A day without a few moments spent worshiping my heavenly Father guarantees that I will be reactive instead of ready to face the day. My schedule doesn't go as planned? A phone call brings bad news? A last-minute e-mail arrives that must be handled above all other tasks? My son's homework assignment requires more time when I should be cooking dinner? My husband needs a listening ear and supportive advice? Without worship, my response to all of these things will likely include a grumpy attitude because I've failed to focus my perspective on what matters most. Worship centers our hearts on God and helps us remember His plan over our expectations. A worshipful heart prepares us for what we may meet in the coming day.

I think Anna knew this. I think that's why she walked through the Beautiful Gate and never looked back. Let's do the same, sister. Imagine Luke were to write a story about our lives today; let's have it start with—"And there was a woman determined to worship God."

Take a moment to fill in your name below as a commitment to the habit of worship:

And there was a woman named _____

who was determined to worship God.

Close your time today by jotting down ways in which you might embrace a worshipful heart. Then spend some time doing just that: ascribe to the Lord the glory due His name. We are never more beautiful than when we are praising Him. Let's start today!

Ways I might embrace a worshipful heart:

DAY 2: FINDING WISDOM IN THE WORD

Look closely at the cover of this book. It's filled with beautiful things: flowers and feathers and berries and branches. All lovely items meant to represent the beauty of the One we are here to learn from. What you see on the cover is not unlike how He is depicted in Isaiah 4:2:

> In that day the Branch of the Lord will be beautiful and glorious, and the fruit of the land will be the pride and glory of the survivors in Israel.

If you'll trace your finger along these lovely details on the cover, you'll find that you are tracing the shape of a circle. Some might call it a wreath, or perhaps more accurately for our assignment today and beyond: a crown.

You can find the image of a crown peppered throughout the Bible. It might designate, as one source explains, "[someone] set apart...for a particular task...high priest or...king...[or simply someone in an] exalted position."[1] A crown might bestow a special honor upon the wearer, a blessing of character, riches, or good harvest. Often in the New Testament, the crown represented a prize to the victor, a lavish garland placed on the winner of a race.[2]

But sometimes the image of a crown represents a slightly different attribute, one that we will seek together today.

Read Luke 2:41-52, and put a placeholder there for future reference.

The Quick Three
What happened?
Where did it happen?
What characters are mentioned in this reading?

Setting the Scene

Twelve years have passed since we last saw Mary, Joseph, and Jesus in the Court of Women with Anna, the determined. The baby Jesus is now a youthful boy, having grown into adolescence in His hometown of Nazareth (Luke 2:39). Like most Jewish families of the day, Mary and Joseph are traveling again to Jerusalem for a specific purpose.

What does Luke 2:41 tell us about why they were journeying to Jerusalem?

The Passover, followed immediately by the Feast of Unleavened Bread, was one of three annual festivals celebrated by the Jews: the Passover and

Extra Insight

According to Jewish custom, biblical manhood began at age thirteen. In today's reading, Jesus was just shy of that by one year. By the age of thirteen, He would be expected to assume adult responsibilities and to know and "follow the Law of Moses."[3] As Numbers 4:46-47 tells us, the traditional age of full manhood would be reached at age thirty, which is the age Jesus was when He began His earthly ministry.

Feast of Unleavened Bread, the Feast of Weeks, and the Feast of Tabernacles or Booths. Each of these festivals required male Jews to travel to Jerusalem, commemorating significant moments of God's provision for the Israelite nation. And often their families would travel with them.

> Exodus 12:24-28 and Deuteronomy 16:1-17 explain the law prompting the Holy Family to travel to Jerusalem for these three feasts. What details do these passages give us about these annual pilgrimages? Make a few notes below:
>
> The Passover and Feast of Unleavened Bread
>
>
> The Feast of Weeks
>
>
> The Feast of Tabernacles or Booths

Imagine a sixty-mile road trip that you embark upon with several hundred of your closest friends and relatives. Now imagine that you are making this road trip via donkey and wagon, with several of you traveling on foot. It would have taken three or four days for the Holy Family to reach Jerusalem in this way.

Once there they celebrate the Lord's great mercy for sparing their people in the first Passover over fourteen hundred years ago, and then they begin the arduous journey back home. But something peculiar happens along the way.

> Summarize Luke 2:43-44 below:

How could Mary and Joseph not know Jesus was with them? Biblical scholar Warren Wiersbe offers this insight, which might help provide an explanation:

> People traveled to the feasts in caravans, the women and children leading the way and setting the pace, and the men and young men following behind. Relatives and whole villages often traveled together and kept an eye on each other's children. At the age of twelve, Jesus could easily have gone from one group to another and not been missed. Joseph would think Jesus was with Mary and the other children, while Mary would suppose He was with Joseph and the men, or perhaps with one of their relatives.[4]

After returning to Jerusalem—frantic, I am sure—where do Mary and Joseph find Jesus? (See Luke 2:46.)

Extra Insight

Glance ahead at Luke 20:1-8, 19 and consider that some of the teachers amazed at twelve-year-old Jesus might be the same ones who will want to kill Him later.

And so, we are back to the Temple courts once more. Not far from where Simeon and Anna held Him and rejoiced at His birth, Jesus sat with the religious teachers having deep discussions in the Temple.

Can you remember a time when God spoke something so clearly that it was impossible to doubt His voice? Perhaps it was a verse that leaped off the pages of the Bible, an answer to a heartfelt prayer, or a gut-conviction that you needed to do something specific in order to obey God. Take a moment to describe what He told you here:

Fast forward a few days, months, or maybe even years. How long did you remember what God told you? Why do you think this was so?

There is a page in my journal where I've recorded several of God's promises in Scripture. Some of the promises I have seen come to pass; some are still yet to happen. Even though I know that God is a keeper of promises, I still have to turn to it often to remind myself of its truth. I easily forget what God has guaranteed.

Why do you think we have a hard time remembering what God has told us?

We have the luxury of reading these two Temple stories recounted in Luke 2:21-39 and Luke 2:41-52 back to back. But twelve years had passed since Mary and Joseph had heard Simeon's prophecy and Anna's praise, and it seems they have forgotten the divine truth uttered in those encounters.

How does Jesus' reply to His parents in Luke 2:49 echo the divine truth shared by Simeon and Anna?

If only Mary and Joseph had remembered! It's easy to hold their memory-retaining ability to a higher standard, but there are more times than I'd like to admit when I have forgotten God's promises and the sound of His voice. If we want to retain what God speaks, we'll have to determine to keep returning to Him. Hold that thought while we take a closer look at Jesus' conversation with the religious leaders.

Amazed at His Understanding

As I am writing this, my son is eleven years old. By the time you hold this study in your hands, he will be twelve, the same age as Jesus in our reading for today. The topics of discussion my son is mostly obsessed with these days are, in no particular order, monkeys, hockey, food, and bathroom visits. Ahem.

I would be quite speechless if he came home from school one day and capably discussed, as one source puts it, "the interpretation of the [Old Testament] law and its implications for both theology and ethics,"[5] but that's exactly the topic of conversation Jesus is having at the Temple with the astonished Jewish teachers.

His reply to His parents gives us an important glimpse into the heart of our Savior.

Rewrite Jesus' reply in Luke 2:49 word for word here:

In two rather profound sentences, Jesus' first recorded spoken words establish two things: (1) that He was the Son of God; and (2) that He came to do His Father's work.

What do these two things reveal about Jesus' priorities, even as a twelve-year-old boy?

Compare the words of Jesus in Luke 2:49 with His words in Luke 4:43; Luke 9:22; and John 3:14. What does Jesus' use of the word *must* in these verses tell us about His commitment to pursuing God's will?

According to Luke 2:52 (NIV), how did Jesus grow as He matured?

Jesus grew in _____ *and* _____, *and in* _____ *with God and man.*

It's the first of these attributes, wisdom, that I want us to focus on today.

Wisdom Is Our Father's Business

When examining the biblical topic of wisdom, the Book of Proverbs offers relevant teaching.

In particular, Proverbs 4:1-13 details the value of wisdom and why we should seek it. Take a few minutes to read these verses and list some of the benefits of gleaning wisdom that are mentioned:

Note the specific benefit mentioned in verse 9 (NIV):

"She will give you a garland to grace your head
and present you with a_____ _____."

Jesus understood that He was put on this earth to do His Father's will. As we walk through this study together, we'll witness Jesus in many necessary encounters before He reached the cross. We should not consider it an accident that the first of these recorded encounters—Jesus in the Temple at age twelve— is a conversation about Old Testament law and Scripture and its implications for godly living.

Note what the following passages tell us about the Hebrew Bible that Jesus would have been familiar with at age twelve:

Luke 24:44

2 Timothy 3:14-15

What does John 1:14 tell us about Jesus and the Word of God?

Extra Insight

Written in Greek and produced in the third and second centuries BC, the Septuagint was "the oldest written translation of the Bible."[6]

The Hebrew Scriptures were Jesus' Bible. He knew them, studied them, valued them, and recited them. What's more, we know from John 1:14 that Jesus was the very Word of God Himself. He understood that knowing the Word of God would be critical in fulfilling the will of God.

Sister, we are diving into the Gospel of Luke together to seek wisdom. There is a very specific path both of us must walk to bring about the plans God has set in motion. You and I have a job to do, and we'll need to retain His Word to see it through. By prioritizing the pursuit of wisdom, we'll take the first step toward accomplishing God's will for our lives.

How do we grow in wisdom?

By prioritizing the pursuit of wisdom, we'll take the first step toward accomplishing God's will for our lives.

1. Choose three verses below to read carefully.
2. Circle the one that resonates most with you today.
3. Rewrite it in your own words in the space below.

Deuteronomy 11:18-23   John 1:1
Joshua 1:8   Ephesians 6:11-17
Psalm 1:2   2 Timothy 3:16-17
Psalm 119:11   James 1:22
Proverbs 3:1-2

My paraphrase:

Are you ready for a high-five? You've already taken the first step. The study of God's Word will shine a bright light on the next step God needs you to take. There is a direct correlation between what we know of God's Word and how well we accomplish God's will. And I'm so glad we are here doing this thing together.

Trace your fingers along the cover of this book once more. Close your eyes and imagine your heavenly Father placing a crown of wisdom upon your head today. And then spend some time in prayer, asking God to flood you with the wisdom of His Word.

If any of you lacks wisdom, you should ask God, who gives generously to all without finding fault, and it will be given to you.

(James 1:5)

DAY 3: A PROMISE TO PRAY

Have you ever had a particular moment when everything changed—when there would be no going back, no do-overs or second chances? There would simply be a new normal with new rules. I have had this experience a few times in my life.

If I were to compare my short list of such moments, the one thing they have in common is that they all marked the definite end of something. The end of a job, the end of a loved one's life, the end of an awareness of something that no longer holds true. And then, change. The end of something is always followed by striking change, and that change is often accompanied by chaos.

Think back to a moment in your life when everything changed.
Consider these questions as you describe it below: What ended?
Did something begin in its place? What were the new rules? How did

you respond to the change? Was there chaos? Was God a part of your response? Was prayer?

I imagine that some of us can look back on our seasons of change and see God's perfect timing in it all. Or maybe your season of change has brought so much disorder and confusion that you can't see the movement of God in it just yet. That's okay. We're here to find Him together.

Today we are going to step into a time in history when there was no scarcity of chaos. Everything was about to change. And as always, even though it looked like things were in an uproar, God's timing in the middle of it all was perfect. These verses summarize this time of change:

> [4]When the set time had fully come, God sent his Son, born of a woman, born under the law, [5]to redeem those under the law, that we might receive adoption to sonship.
>
> (Galatians 4:4-5)

With this backdrop, we're ready to jump into our passage for today.

Read Luke 3:1-23, and put a placeholder there for future reference.

The Quick Three
What happened?
Where did it happen?
What characters are mentioned in this reading?

Setting the Scene

I don't know if you noticed, but Luke throws a lot of characters at us in the first two verses of our reading. That's intentional. If you'll glance back at Luke 3:1-4 to see Luke's objective in writing this Gospel, you'll see that he wants his reader to understand the world he is describing in detail. So before we continue any further, let's try to make sense of the five rulers and two high priests Luke mentions.

Reread Luke 3:1-2 and fill in the blank boxes in the chart.[1]

Character	Job	Reign	Notes
	Emperor of the Roman Empire	AD 14–37	Succeeded Octavian Augustus Caesar
Pontius Pilate		AD 26–36	Will appear later in Luke 23 during Jesus' trial and crucifixion.
	Tetrarch* of Galilee and Perea	4 BC–AD 39	Son of Herod the Great; See Luke 1:5
Philip		4 BC–AD 34	Son of Herod the Great
	Tetrarch of Abilene	Specific dates unknown, but during the reign of Tiberius Caesar	Abilene was north of Mount Hermon
Annas		AD 6–15	Caiaphus's father-in -law; See Acts 4:6
Caiaphas		AD 18–36	Annas's son-in-law
*Tetrarch = "the governor of a region"[2]			

The third chapter of Luke takes us to around AD 28–29, and although the Greek Empire had conquered much of the world a few centuries prior, the Roman Empire was now in control of Palestine. Between the mingling of Greek and Roman cultures, along with a myriad of different groups of Jews, we can rightly imagine a vibrant melting pot of languages, beliefs, and priorities as leaders within these factions challenged one another for political prominence.[3]

There are two words that come to mind when considering each of the political leaders we've just charted together: *soap opera*. I'm not joking. Understanding their roles and responsibilities is one feat; understanding their behavior choices is another challenge altogether. As Charles Swindoll has observed, just among the seven characters named above there is murder, adultery, jealousy, insatiable greed, incest, exile, and cruelty.[4] He writes of this bleak time in history: "John began his ministry during a time of political fracturing in Israel. While priests and procurators vied for power, the people desperately longed for a leader."[5]

Sounds like chaos, right? And into this divided political climate entered John the Baptist, who was the son of Zechariah, cousin of Jesus, prophet of God, and undoubtedly a societal misfit living in the wilderness. We've considered the political climate at this time, but what about general society?

Based on the questions the crowd asks of John and his responses in Luke 3:7-14, how would you describe the cultural climate of the day? How do you think the people of first-century Israel treated one another?

And into this swirling cultural climate entered the Son of God.

The Opening of Heaven

The first-century world was about to change, and the crowds in the wilderness that day knew it. Let's find out why.

Take a look at Luke 3:21-22. What was Jesus doing, and what happened as He did this?

Read the words of the Old Testament prophet Ezekiel in Ezekiel 1:1. What happened after the heavens were opened?

I have several notification sounds programmed into my smart phone. One sound notifies me of updates within certain apps, one signals an approaching thunderstorm, and one tells me that my phone battery is about to die. They all sound different, but the notification that sounds like a bell tells me that I have a new incoming text message. I know when I hear that particular bell that someone is trying to communicate with me.

The opening of heaven described by both Luke and the prophet Ezekiel served in a similar way as a notification. In each instance, divine communication followed. The opened heavens were God's way of saying, "Listen up! Pay attention! I am about to speak!" This moment described in Luke 3:21 was an especially unique circumstance considering that the Israelites had not received direct communication from God in about four hundred years.[7] *Everything was about to change*.

You'll recall that Jesus was praying as heaven was opened. Three other things happened as Jesus was praying.

Review Luke 3:21-22 and fill in the blanks that follow:

Jesus prayed and...heaven opened.

Extra Insight

John taught a "baptism of repentance for the forgiveness of sins" (Luke 3:3). If Jesus was the faultless Son of God, why was His baptism necessary? Scholars have varying opinions on this, but Jesus gave his answer in Matthew 3:14-15.

Extra Insight

If you compare the Gospel of Luke with the Gospels of Matthew, Mark, and John, you'll find that Luke portrays Jesus in prayer more often than any other Gospel author.[6] You can also find Jesus at prayer in Luke 5:16, 6:12, 9:18, 9:28-29, 11:1, 22:41-44, 23:34, and 23:46.

Extra Insight

Luke 3:21-22 records the appearance of the Trinity together: the Father, the Son, and the Holy Spirit.

the _____ _____ descended.

a _____ came from heaven (the voice of God Himself).

Jesus was declared as God's _____.

Do you think it was a coincidence that these things happened as Jesus was praying? Why or why not?

After all these remarkable things happened as Jesus prayed, something just as remarkable was about to begin.

Luke 3:23 records the start of something that changed everything. What was it?

A Commitment to Prayer

As we continue through our study of Luke, we'll see Jesus at prayer regularly; but this first observance of Him in communication with His Father is not a minor one. Big things happened after Jesus prayed here. It marked the end of a silent era for the people of God and the beginning of His ministry to the entire world. Jesus' prayer paved the way for the movement of God. As I think of the Savior of the world on His knees before the start of something that changed everything, I have to ask myself if I am as committed to prayer as He was.

Do you have a habit of prayer? Is it consistent? Sporadic? Heartfelt? Need-based? Jot a few words below to describe your current prayer life.

If what you just described didn't include words such as *consistent*, *rewarding*, or *regular*, let me ask you this: what would it take for you to start defining prayer as *required*? Not in the sense of an expectation or obligation but in the sense of a necessity for daily life. What perspective shift do you need in order to move the habit of prayer from a rote behavior you are simply checking off the list to an absolute necessity for your potential to thrive as a follower of Jesus?

Last year my husband and I committed to daily prayer together over our son's schooling choices. We thought we might be praying over this decision for a few weeks, but God had another time line in mind. A few *months* later, as we were still praying over the decision, the rich rewards of our commitment became evident:

1. **Daily prayer is a constant reminder that God is in control**. Even though we are walking into the unknown, the habit of continually bringing our hearts to God soothes anxiety and worry that might threaten to creep in. Comfort is found in our daily pause to acknowledge that God's ways are higher than ours.
2. **A prayerful heart is a thankful heart**. What began as a request for answers turned into an outpouring of gratitude. As Tom and I waited for God to reveal Himself, God grew an attitude of thankfulness in us both. The language of our prayers shifted from "God we need this answer please" to "God you have blessed us so."
3. **Prayer gives birth to emotional intimacy**. Prayer connects us to the people with whom we are praying. I look forward to my prayer time with Tom because I know it will be precious time spent together. If you want to build a closer bond with someone, praying together is a wonderful way to start.

> A commitment to prayer increases intimacy with our heavenly Father.

It's this last reward that echoes in my mind as I read of Jesus' prayer and the heavens opening in Luke 3. Prayer draws us close to our heavenly Father because it's how we communicate with Him. A commitment to prayer increases intimacy with our heavenly Father.

Like the divine communication following the opening of the heavens, we can know that the deepening of our relationship with God will follow the bowing of our heads in prayer. And that changes everything.

Spend some time in prayer as we close out this day, perhaps writing your thoughts in the margin as you pray. Ask Jesus to give you a heart that yearns for prayer because you yearn for Him.

DAY 4: AN OBLIGATION TO OBEY

There is a purpose to my pain. I often whisper this to myself in seasons of hardship, whether I believe it in the moment or not. When we're in the middle of such a moment, in a place that feels like either a test or a temptation, it's difficult to imagine that anything good might follow. Our eyes can only see what's right in front of us, and maintaining the awareness that there is value in hardship requires patience and a perspective we don't readily choose. We are human, after all.

But again and again, God's Word reminds us that the pain we experience today can be used to prepare us for our godly designed purpose. So the question remains: How do we bridge the gap between what we see and what lies ahead—between the pain of today and the hope found in tomorrow? The moments between these two are where our faith is built; and if we want to please God, we'll have to hold them with reverent hands.

We'll find the way to do that today by looking to the One who was both fully divine and fully human. He understands our pain and knows that the path to finding our purpose is marked with obedience.

> I will hasten and not delay
> to obey your commands.
> (Psalm 119:60)

Read Luke 4:1-13, and put a placeholder there for future reference.

The Quick Three
What happened?
Where did it happen?
What characters are mentioned in this reading?

Setting the Scene

As you'll recall from Luke 3:23, which we read yesterday, Jesus was about to launch His ministry. Think for a moment about the launch of a new business, a new product, a new church, or a new campaign. If you were managing such a launch, you would want the public to know. There would be announcements. Advertisements. Brochures to send to interested individuals. Parties, even. As we consider that this is the beginning of Jesus' earthly ministry, we might assume this would be the perfect time for Him to go public. Instead we find Him going into the wilderness.

What does Luke 4:1-2 tell us about His experience in the wilderness?

Carefully consider Hebrews 2:14-18. Based on what this tells us, why might the Spirit have led Jesus into this encounter?

There is a purpose to Jesus' pain in the wilderness. Here God is preparing Him to come to our aid when we need it the most. Not unlike those who undergo first aid training to assist someone in medical crisis, Jesus undergoes humanity training in the wilderness to assist us in a spiritual crisis. His experience here enables Him to understand our plight and proclaims that He is worthy to redeem it:

> We do not have a high priest who is unable to empathize with our weaknesses, but we have one who has been tempted in every way, just as we are—yet he did not sin.
>
> (Hebrews 4:15)

But there is more to this scene that is unfolding. As we see Jesus fasting, hungry, and alone, Luke sets forth the entire premise of Jesus' ministry. Charles Swindoll writes that our passage for today "sets the tone for the rest of Luke's Gospel, which is essentially an account of the war between the Son of God and Satan."[1] There is a battle waging between good and evil, and Jesus has come to end it.

The Three P's of the Wilderness

Luke tells us in verse 13 of chapter 4 that the devil tempted Jesus in every possible way, but he describes three of them in detail. Let's consider them together.

The first temptation

How is Jesus tempted in Luke 4:3-4?

Circle the phrase that describes this temptation:

To doubt God's provision

To desire God's power

To embrace selfish pride

The devil knows that Jesus is hungry, and he tempts Jesus to doubt that God will provide for His physical needs.

Can you think of a moment of hardship when you were afraid your needs would not be met? How did you react or communicate with God in that moment?

How did Jesus respond to the devil?

The second temptation

How is Jesus tempted in Luke 4:5-8?

Circle the phrase that describes this temptation:

To doubt God's provision

To desire God's power

To embrace selfish pride

The devil is the prince of the world (John 12:31), and he tempts Jesus with the lie that what the world offers is greater than what God offers.

Can you think of a moment of hardship when you were tempted to put something worldly before God? How did you react or communicate with God in that moment?

How did Jesus respond to the devil?

The third temptation

How is Jesus tempted in Luke 4:9-12?

Circle the phrase that describes this temptation:

To doubt God's provision

To desire God's power

To embrace selfish pride

The devil recognizes Jesus as the Son of God, fully divine and capable of saving Himself, and he tempts Jesus with the prideful lie that He doesn't need God.

Can you think of a moment of hardship when you were tempted to believe that you could do it all on your own? How did you react or communicate with God in that moment?

How did Jesus respond to the devil?

Extra Insight

The devil subtlety misquotes Scripture in Luke 4:10. Compare this verse with Psalm 91:11 to see what he left out.

In each of these temptations, Jesus responds with wisdom from Scripture, saying "It is written…"

If you were to tell how Jesus responded to the devil in all of these temptations with a summary of just a few words, what would you say?

I like to think on the following words when referring to the example Jesus sets for us here: *Jesus obeyed His Father.* In the throes of hunger, Jesus obeyed. When enticed with worldly power, Jesus obeyed. When seduced to engage his ego, Jesus obeyed. When we are in a place of hardship that feels like either a test or a temptation, we can remember that Jesus has shown us the way out. The way to bridge the gap between what we see and what lies ahead is found in the simple act of obeying our heavenly Father.

Daughters of the Creator

Consider for a moment the thought patterns running through your head during seasons of hardship. Not the ones you tell your best friend. The ones you keep to yourself. The thoughts you're afraid to say out loud. The patterns you might not even be able to articulate clearly.

Do any of them resemble the following statements?

- God won't take care of my needs.
- This thing that the world offers is better than what God offers.
- I can do this on my own. I don't need Jesus to save me.

If so, take a moment to confess these thoughts to the Lord. Write a brief prayer in the margin, if you want:

I've experienced each of these thought patterns during my faith journey. When I was finally able to apply some hindsight to the fallacy of these lies, what hurt the most wasn't that I had believed them. It was that I had let them separate me from God.

Look closer at the enemy's end goal. While it may seem that the devil's sole aim is to entice Jesus into disobeying God's written commands, what he is really after is to alter Jesus' perfect relationship with His heavenly Father. And Jesus will have no part in it because the Father and the Son are not meant to be separated. Instead, He shows us that the way to preserve our relationship with God is to obey His will for our lives. This isn't about works over faith. This is about doing what God tells us to do because He loves us as His children and we are meant to be in relationship with Him.

Twice the devil refers to Jesus as the Son of God, not only acknowledging Jesus' divinity but also showing that He is beloved family to God Himself. Only Jesus can emerge from temptation unscathed and still holy. Biblical commentator R. T. France suggests that this is Luke's primary purpose in sharing this encounter: to prove that Jesus is the holy and righteous Son of God.[3]

Our faith walk will require consistent requests for forgiveness, even as we are made more and more like Jesus. We will not be perfected until we see Him face to face. But, sister, we are part of that same family. In Romans 8 we read, "If we are children, then we are heirs—heirs of God and co-heirs with Christ, if indeed we share in his sufferings in order that we may also share in his glory" (v. 17). We are the daughters of the Creator of the universe. Our response to both tests and temptations should be just like that of Jesus. We overcome the enemy's attempts to separate us from God when we determine to obey God's will.

Just as this experience helped to prepare Jesus for His earthly ministry, so seasons of hardship can prepare us to move forward in God's will for our lives.

How do we determine to obey?

1. Remember that just as the devil pursued Jesus when he was hungry and alone, we can expect to be tempted when we are weak and isolated.
2. Be ready to respond with truth from the Word. We cannot be obedient to what we do not know.
3. Don't give up. Keep applying God's truth to our hard places, being determined to obey God over and over again.

Let's close by penning a prayer to Jesus. I'll get us started and you can continue it with your own words as you are led. If you are walking through a season of hardship right now, write it in the blank below and allow God's grace to wash over you as you pray these words:

Jesus, I know You understand what it feels like to be led into the wilderness. I know You understand what it feels like to be tempted in every way. Thank You for walking through these moments of hardship so that You can guide me through mine. There can be purpose in my

_____ _____, because You can use it prepare me for what is to come. Help me trust in You as I walk through this season.

> We overcome the enemy's attempts to separate us from God when we determine to obey God's will.

DAY 5: DETERMINED PATTERNS OF FAITH

In 1517, a local professor of biblical studies walked up to the Wittenberg church in Germany and hung a document on its door. His name? Martin Luther. His document, known as the "Ninety-Five Theses," would be translated into German and published for the general public, where it would become the foundation of one of the largest revolutions known to church history. We know it as the Protestant Reformation.[1]

The humble document posted to the Wittenberg church door was Luther's manifesto, a public declaration proclaiming why he believed what he believed and what he was going to do about it.

It wasn't the first time a religious leader publicly declared his mission to the world.

In an ordinary Nazarene synagogue, surrounded by those who had watched Him grow in wisdom and stature and in favor with God and men, our Savior did the same.

Read Luke 4:14-30, and put a placeholder there for future reference.

The Quick Three
What happened?
Where did it happen?
What characters are mentioned in this reading?

Setting the Scene

When we read of Jesus returning to Galilee, His ministry has already begun. His early actions are recorded in John 1:19–4:45, but Luke wants his readers to begin here, in Jesus' hometown of Nazareth. Like any faithful Jewish worshiper of the day, Jesus attends regular services at the synagogue on the Sabbath.

One source explains that a typical first-century synagogue service would have looked like this:

1. Invocation for God's blessing
2. Recitation of the traditional Hebrew confession of faith, found in Deuteronomy 6:4-9 and Deuteronomy 11:13-21

3. Prayer
4. Readings from the Law and from the Prophets
5. Brief sermon
6. Closing benediction, if a priest was present. If not, a layman would pray and dismiss the meeting.[2]

Recall from Day 3 of our study this week that Jesus is beginning His ministry during a time of political turmoil for Israel. Like Anna and Simeon, whom we met earlier in the Jerusalem Temple, some Jewish listeners still hear the Minor Prophets of the Old Testament echoing in their minds and are eagerly anticipating the coming Messiah. One source notes that others are hungry for a charismatic leader who might overthrow the Roman empire.[3]

Another commentator notes that many in Nazareth would remember the destruction of the nearby city of Sepphoris by the Roman army in response to a Jewish rebel uprising. Tensions were high. Messianic announcements and anything pertaining to the plight of the Jewish nation were not received with indifference.[4]

And so enters the Messiah Himself as the designated speaker for the synagogue service on this particular day.

The Messianic Manifesto

According to Luke 4:17, what scroll of the Hebrew Scriptures was handed to Jesus?

We don't know whether this particular passage was chosen because it was from a predetermined schedule of Scripture readings in the synagogue for that day or because Jesus selected it Himself.[5] But Jesus reads the words recorded in Isaiah 61:1-2, which were spoken about the coming Messiah. The Messiah had indeed come, and He wanted to make clear His purpose. We can never accuse Jesus of being ambivalent or unintentional. In fact, from the onset of His ministry, Jesus is quite determined about His mission.

What was His specific mission? Let's explore it together.

Read Luke 4:18-19 (NIV if possible), and fill in the blanks to indicate what five things the Spirit of the Lord anointed Jesus to do:

To proclaim _____ _____ to the poor

To proclaim _____ for the prisoners

To proclaim _____ of _____ for the blind

To set the _____ free

To proclaim the year of the _____ _____

These two verses hold Jesus' manifesto. Everything that He would accomplish in His earthly ministry would be done with these five things in mind. He was determined to fulfill His purpose from the start, and let's not gloss over the fact that even then He had His mind set on *you*.

Of the five intentions Jesus mentioned, which one resonates most with you today? Why?

Describe the initial response of Jesus' hometown listeners in Luke 4:22.

Now describe their later response in Luke 4:28.

What caused the reversal in their response? The clues are found in the stories Jesus tells in Luke 4:25-27, which are recorded in full in 1 Kings 17:7-24 and 2 Kings 5:1-14. Read the Scriptures and complete the chart below.

	1 Kings 17:7-24	2 Kings 5:1-14
What prophet is mentioned in this passage?		
Who does he minister to?		
How was the favor of the Lord given?		
From where is the person who received the Lord's favor?	(Luke 4:26)	(Luke 4:27)

Extra Insight

Luke 4:23 makes mention of acts that Jesus had already done in Capernaum. These "events recorded in John 1:19–4:45 took place at this time, but Matthew, Mark, and Luke did not record them."[6]

Of all the stories from the past that Jesus could tell that day, He chose these two for a reason. As one source notes, "Both Sidon and Syria were traditional enemies of Israel."[7] This means that both Zarephath and Naaman were Gentiles. As He preached to the crowd of hometown listeners, Jesus was not painting a picture of God's privileged favor upon the nation of Israel. Jesus' mission was radical: He had come to save the entire world. Both Jews and Gentiles were invited to be part of the kingdom of God, but this was not what the people of

Extra Insight

A Gentile was any person not in the Jewish nation or faith. As one writer notes, "The Messiah didn't come to rescue only one particular race; He came to save those who wanted a Savior. His domain is the whole world, and His subjects are all those who call Him King."[9]

Nazareth wanted to hear. One commentary notes that Jesus' listeners expected to be saved because of their ancestry, not their faith, and they preferred exclusivity over the acceptance of Gentiles.[8]

How do the synagogue listeners act upon their anger in Luke 4:29?

Scripture doesn't tell us how Jesus evaded His first murder attempt. Luke just tells us that He moves on, determined to fulfill the mission He so clearly articulated to the crowd that now wants to kill him.

Read Luke 4:30 and describe how Jesus might have been feeling.

Habits for Success

Jesus, I don't want to waste my time on earth. Teach me to choose determined living so that I can make a difference for your Kingdom with the days that remain.

This was my prayer after receiving a diagnosis of Vascular Ehlers-Danlos Syndrome. Living with a condition that threatens the spontaneous rupture of blood vessels, arteries, and organs has taught me that life is precious. Every choice matters. A yes to one thing now means a no to something else later. And none of our yeses will make any difference at all if they are not grounded in God's will for our life.

What we are studying together is the central truth God taught me about determined living: Jesus did it first. His is the only example we need to follow. One of the questions I asked of God as I considered the choices that Jesus made on His way to the cross was this: Is there a sustainable template for daily living that would produce the maximum impact for His kingdom?

In these first few chapters of Luke, I think we've found it.

Glance back at your homework from this week and summarize in your own words what we've learned so far:

Day 1: Anna was determined to worship.

Day 2: We can find the wisdom of Jesus in God's Word.

Day 3: A commitment to prayer increases intimacy with our heavenly Father.

Day 4: Jesus thwarts the enemy's attempts to separate Him from God by obeying God's will.

Worship. Word. Pray. Obey. These are our habits for success. This is our sustainable template for daily, determined living. If we want to live like Jesus, we will seek to engage in these actions every day.

We have seen Jesus display His manifesto in today's reading. But what about ours?

If you know your God-given purpose in life, describe it here:

A year ago, I would have responded to that question by telling you that God has called me to women's ministry as a Bible study writer and teacher. But I am telling you today that my response isn't exactly accurate. What God has called me to is this: to glorify His name by spending time with Him, reading His Word, talking to Him in prayer, and worshiping His faithfulness. And out of the overflow of that obedience comes the fulfillment of God's will for my life. The details may vary from season to season, but the ultimate goal of glorifying God remains. The same is true for you.

Read these verses and describe in your own words what each says or implies about our God-given purpose:

Proverbs 16:9

Isaiah 43:7

Ephesians 2:10

We will fulfill our purpose on earth when we routinely display patterns of determined faithfulness.

God isn't looking for perfect people who know how to do everything right. He's looking for people who are willing to choose habits of faithfulness. He will direct the outpouring of our time spent with Him to spill over where it needs to.

This is our manifesto as emulators of Jesus: Worship. Word. Pray. Obey. We will fulfill our purpose on earth when we routinely display these patterns of determined faithfulness.

Let's close out this week by acknowledging the ways in which we already do this and noting areas where we can deepen our determination. In every day, how do you or how can you:

Worship God?

Study His Word?

Pray to Him?

Obey what He says?

Sister, I am so proud of you! More important, so is your heavenly Father. You are displaying patterns of faithfulness right now and are well on your way to determined living. Next week Jesus has much to teach us about God's kingdom. Until then, let's live like Jesus in every day: worship, word, pray, and obey.

VIDEO VIEWER GUIDE: WEEK 1

Luke 1:67-79

Luke 2:14

Because Jesus was determined to choose life for us, we can
_____ _____ with Him even when we are walking
through darkness.

John 10:10

The path of peace is not found by _____ _____.

We are changed by the _____ we make and only Jesus can help
us make the right ones.

Luke 1:37

Week 2

The Teacher

Determined to
Demonstrate a New Way

(Luke 4–6)

> ¹In the beginning was the Word, and the Word was with God, and the Word was God. ²He was with God in the beginning. ³Through him all things were made; without him nothing was made that has been made. ⁴In him was life, and that life was the light of all mankind.
> (John 1:1-4)

I taught preschool music for several years, and the stories I came home with were priceless. There's nothing like watching a room full of three- and four-year-olds trying to navigate the world while simultaneously operating musical instruments.

I wasn't particularly qualified for early childhood education. I loved children and had studied music in college. That was the extent of my competence. We had fun together, and the children learned to express themselves through music; but I would never be considered an authority on preschool music education.

Jesus was many things to the people of first-century Israel: Messiah, Savior, healer, friend, hometown hero, agitator, rescuer, miracle worker, and victor. But He was also a teacher—and He taught with authority and expertise. At the heart of His ministry was the intention to teach the world a new way to live. He knew the way because He was the way.

As we begin our study for this week, we will see His observers express amazement at His authority. Not unlike my sweet preschool students, the people of Israel were accustomed to religious teachers who simply reiterated what someone else had told them. No one spoke as an authority; they were mouthpieces to wisdom that had been handed down from heaven generations before.

And then heaven came down and changed everything. Jesus taught with authority because He was the original author. He Himself was the Word.

As students of the Bible, we are receiving the truth straight from the source: Jesus Christ. The original language from the opening verses in Luke 4:31-32 describes Jesus as one who held the "sovereign, authoritative decision of a king or a judge."[1] We can trust that what we are about to learn from Him will be transformative.

Not only was Jesus the author of what He was teaching; what He taught was a new way. It was life—determined living—and it wasted nothing. Gone were the days of drifting and wandering and waiting. The kingdom of God had finally come.

You and I are a part of that Kingdom! Let's walk in this new way together.

DAY 1: A SOLITARY PLACE

Walk a mile in their shoes. If you want to truly understand a person, this is sound advice. Each of us brings a unique set of backgrounds, experiences, and beliefs that influence the choices we make. Following footsteps that aren't familiar to us drenches us in a different perspective.

And perspective matters. It removes the filter of what we think we see and replaces it with understanding. It can mean the difference between delivering judgment or grace. A healthy dose of it can quickly turn criticism into empathy and it will often turn a foe into a friend.

It's the details of that perspective that make a difference, however. We might think we already know a particular set of footsteps but examining the details of its path might shed light on behaviors and decisions that we hadn't considered yet, but probably should. Adopting details from the right perspective can change our course for the better.

Today, we are going to walk a mile in Jesus' shoes on a typical day during His ministry. Well, technically, we'll walk a few miles. There are details to notice along the way because His perspective is one that we want to embrace. I'll go ahead and give you a spoiler alert though: from sunup to sundown, He is determined.

Read Luke 4:31-44, and put a placeholder there for future reference.

The Quick Three
What happened?
Where did it happen?
What characters are mentioned in this reading?

Setting the Scene

Jesus spent His time on earth traveling between Galilee, Samaria, and Judea. After being rejected in His hometown of Nazareth, which was located in Galilee, Jesus settled into Capernaum as His headquarters for much of His ministry.[1]

Rasmussen's *Atlas of the Bible* tells us that Capernaum was a bustling city. Nestled on the northwestern shore of the Sea of Galilee, it lay along an international route that ran from the Mediterranean Sea to Transjordan and

Damascus. Many of its inhabitants were likely fishermen, including Jesus' first disciples. He was in Capernaum when He found them (Matthew 4:18-22).[2]

It is here in Capernaum that we begin a typical day in the life of the Savior of the world, who was always on mission.

Consider your daily obligations for this week. Would you define your schedule as busy, relaxed, or somewhere in between?

To say that Jesus had an active day in Capernaum would be an understatement. List in order the sequence of events for His day found in Luke 4:31-41:

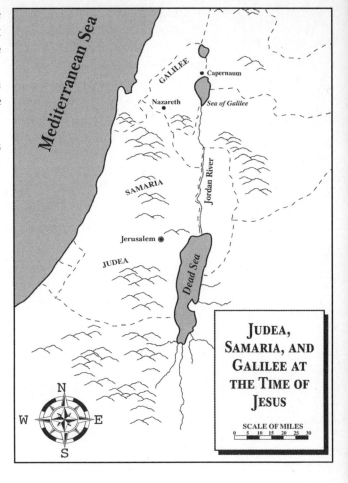

Mediterranean Sea

GALILEE

Capernaum

Nazareth

Sea of Galilee

SAMARIA

Jordan River

Jerusalem

JUDEA

Dead Sea

JUDEA, SAMARIA, AND GALILEE AT THE TIME OF JESUS

SCALE OF MILES
0   5   10   15   20   25   30

N
W   E
S

Let's take a closer look at the different types of encounters Jesus experienced. Read and respond to each section below:

Luke 4:31-32–Mental (teaching)
What does this encounter teach us about Jesus?

Luke 4:33-37–Supernatural (exorcism)
What does this encounter teach us about Jesus?

Luke 4:38-39–Physical (healing)
What does this encounter teach us about Jesus?

Luke 4:40-41–Extended ministry work
What does this encounter teach us about Jesus?

Based on the work in which Jesus engaged, place a check mark beside the objectives you think He was committed to:

___ teaching the truth

___ eradicating the source of evil

___ restoring the brokenness caused by evil

___ all of the above

How do Jesus' actions in Capernaum from today's reading align with His manifesto from Isaiah that we read last week in Luke 4:18-19 (page 36)?

Jesus was always on mission. In Scripture we never see Him engaging in activities that do not fully support His purpose. Behind every encounter and behind every choice was a Savior who was determined to love the world. Nothing He does is accidental, including His choice to walk away from the noise.

Recall the last time you sought out physical, mental, and emotional renewal. Describe what that looked like for you and how you felt afterward:

Where does Jesus go in Luke 4:42?

Why do you think He seeks solitude?

Luke doesn't tell us here what Jesus does in that solitary place. But Luke 5:16 and 6:12 give us clues. Read both of these verses and describe Jesus' behavior:

Extra Insight

Jewish laws prohibited work on the Sabbath; this included the physical job of carrying the sick to be healed. Biblical commentator R. T. France notes that the Sabbath ended when the sun went down, prompting the crowd to bring those in need of healing to Jesus in droves. He also reminds us that we'll see Jesus' acts of healing on the Sabbath provoke controversy later in Luke.[3]

Although He was completely divine, Jesus laid His divinity down so that He might understand what it felt like to be fully human. Humans get tired. Jesus understands that. When we are tempted to think that no one could possibly understand how stressed out, exhausted, or weary we are, we can follow Jesus' footsteps to solitude. In the midst of a busy day, one that required the constant pouring out of energy and knowledge and love, Jesus knew that in order to continue His mission He would have to stop and renew His strength.

This detail of His day gives us valuable perspective. It's one that I often skip over when I read the Gospels. Yes, Jesus taught the truth. He exerted authority over evil. He healed those who were sick. But He also intentionally sought time away from the crowd that pursued Him. If the holy and perfect Son of God sought out solitary places for spiritual renewal, how much more should this be a priority for us?

How high of a priority is spiritual renewal in your life? Circle the answer that is most appropriate for you today:

I take it when I am forced to.

If there is space in my day once I see to my other obligations, then I will seek rest and renewal.

I am proactive about scheduling downtime. I know I won't be nearly as productive without it.

The Difference Between Good and Best

We live in a culture of noise. Television, radio, podcasts, and every social media platform on the planet are all screaming for our attention. Most of us have more media devices in our homes than we do people. Even some gas stations deliver audiovisual ads while we wait for the fuel to pump into our cars. Silence is a precious and rare commodity.

As it was with Jesus, our fruitfulness is determined by our willingness to seek spiritual rest and renewal with our Father.

If we aren't intentional about turning off the noise and seeking spiritual renewal, we won't be able to continue our mission. As it was with Jesus, our fruitfulness is determined by our willingness to seek spiritual rest and renewal with our Father.

Since we are after determined living, let's get practical and apply this to both our short-term and long-term schedules.

Take a few moments to consider your weekly schedule. In the margin or on a separate piece of paper, list the obligations you have and the people who rely on you. Pray over what you have written, surrendering your commitments to Jesus. Then ask Him to give you wisdom about times you can reserve for spiritual renewal. Shade in those areas below.

	MON	TUE	WED	THU	FRI	SAT	SUN
Morning							
Afternoon							
Evening							

If you keep a weekly calendar, go ahead and block out the times you shaded above in your calendar as well. You might even label them as WWPO time—*Worship. Word. Pray. Obey.* Protect these scheduled times as you would an important appointment. Expect interruptions, but don't give in to them. Don't let last-minute obligations keep you from spending time with Jesus. These will be the most important appointments you will keep all week.

Now consider your monthly schedule. Think about your work obligations, your family routines and commitments, school schedules, travel plans, and holidays. In the chart below, place an X over the months that will be the busiest. These are the months when you get to practice saying no. Acknowledge that these are already going to be busy months, and determine not to add new obligations to them.

Circle the months that have a little more margin in them. These are the months when you can seek opportunities for deeper renewal, such as a family vacation, a planned staycation, or a spiritual retreat with friends or alone. The goal is to set your mind to it now, viewing time away from the noise of our day-to-day lives as a priority.

January	February	March	April
May	June	July	August
September	October	November	December

When we acknowledge spiritual rest as an important detail that Jesus refused to neglect, our capacity to emulate His love for the world will increase.

Here are a few final words from one over-committer to another. Know your own limits. Also know that your limits won't look like someone else's limits, and that's okay. My husband's extroverted personality allows him to sustain longer periods of interaction with others, while I need more rest and downtime. Neither capacity is better than the other; they are simply reflections of God's creativity in designing people. Be confident in the way God made you so that you can acknowledge your unique needs and be wise enough to let God meet them. Remember, carving out space for spiritual renewal helps us to listen to God's voice with clarity, deepen our intimacy with Him, determine His will for our lives, and find strength to obey it.

In the last two verses of today's reading, we see Jesus doing just that: obeying His Father's will. Describe Jesus' attitude expressed in Luke 4:43-44:

There's that word *must* again. One commentator suggests that Jesus knew the difference between what was good and what was best.[4] Of course, it would have been *good* if He had stayed and healed more people in Capernaum. Based on the crowd's demeanor, it certainly would have been *popular*. But it wouldn't have been the *best*. His best was bringing the kingdom of God to the entire world. Jesus knew His mission, and He was determined to see it through. End your time today by praying for the ability to follow His example.

Jesus, my time on earth is precious. Teach me how to spend it well. Give me foresight to reserve time with You for rest and renewal, remembering that I must remain in You if I am to bear fruit (John 15:5). Give me wisdom to know the difference between what is good and what is best. Then give me strength to rise and obey Your will. Amen.

DAY 2: STRENGTH IN NUMBERS

The water on the pond glistened in the afternoon light. It was still and quiet, and were it not for the gentle breeze that caught the end of my pigtails every now and then, I would almost have thought we were walking into a painting instead of the field across the street. He knew the way through the thicket, and I tried to match my first-grade footsteps to his as we walked to the clearing that held our footprints from the day before. Our feathered friends sang to us along the way, and he would quietly tell me their names without having to look at the bird itself. *Mockingjay. Whippoorwill. Swallow.* My grandfather was a good listener.

Extra Insight

Luke 4:43 is the first reference to the "kingdom of God" in the Gospel of Luke.

"I am the vine; you are the branches. If you remain in me and I in you, you will bear much fruit; apart from me you can do nothing."

(John 15:5)

We reached the edge of the water, and he set down the fishing poles as I set down his toolbox. Slowly and methodically, he readied each hook with bait. I looked out onto the still water and scrunched my forehead.

"Papa, how do you know the fish are still in there?"

"They're always there. You just have to seek them out."

"Won't that be a lot of work? That's a small worm, and this is a big pond."

"That's why you're here to help me."

My grandfather taught me a lot about fishing. His pond was small, but the principles are the same no matter what body of water you are gleaning from. Fish hide in the deep waters to stay cool during the day. The best time to find them in the shallow end is at night. And yet, it is into the deep waters in the middle of the day that Jesus calls Simon, the fisherman.

Read Luke 5:1-11, and put a placeholder there for future reference.

The Quick Three
What happened?
Where did it happen?
What characters are mentioned in this reading?

Setting the Scene

Luke 5:1 tells us that Jesus was teaching at the Lake of Gennesaret, which is simply another name for the Sea of Galilee. Commentator Craig Keener notes that fishermen were abundantly found near its shores and they were accustomed to working in teams. The cost of fishing equipment was high and the labor was physically demanding, so collaborating boosted their profits.[1]

What is Jesus doing in Luke 5:3?

Is He in shallow waters or deep?

This isn't the first time Simon Peter, James, and John have met Jesus. How does verse 5 imply that Simon is familiar with Jesus' authority? What does Simon Peter call Jesus in this verse?

Used only in Luke's Gospel in reference to Jesus, the word *Master* refers to "those who have been put in charge, officials, overseers, and rulers."[2] We find Simon Peter meeting Jesus for the first time in John 1:40-42 and witnessing Jesus heal his mother-in-law in Luke 4:38-39. So here in Luke 5 he is familiar with Jesus' authority, which might explain why he obeys when Jesus calls him into the deep.

The Five Characteristics of Discipleship

Luke's use of the term *Master* was fitting; Jesus was the authority over all things, including discipleship. As we seek to emulate Him, we will learn best from those who have mastered this same intention.

Do you have someone in your life you consider to be a Christian mentor? Are you actively involved in shaping someone else's faith journey—a mentee? If so, take a moment to describe these people and your relationships with them. If not, jot down the names of two people who might fill these roles.

The word *disciple* is used many times in the Gospel of Luke, although he does not introduce the word formally until Luke 5:30. As we continue our study of Luke, we will watch Jesus build His ministry upon the foundation of discipleship. Matthew records some of Jesus' last words to His disciples, commanding them to make new disciples throughout all nations:

[19]*"Go and make disciples of all nations, baptizing them in the name of the Father and of the Son and of the Holy Spirit,* [20]*and teaching them to obey everything I have commanded you. And surely I am with you always, to the very end of the age."*
(Matthew 28:19-20)

Luke chooses to give discipleship a place of prominence by recording it as one of the earliest actions Jesus takes to grow His ministry.

How would you define *disciple* in your own words?

Today's Scripture reading shows us five things we can learn about discipleship from Jesus. Let's examine them together.

1. *Ordinary individuals can jump to the front of the line when it comes to disicipleship.*

When they saw the courage of Peter and John and realized that they were unschooled, ordinary men, they were astonished and they took note that these men had been with Jesus.

(Acts 4:13)

Simon, James, and John were not religious teachers or political leaders; they were ordinary fishermen. If there was any doubt as to whether Jesus' called disciples were qualified, Luke defends their role in Acts 4:13 (see "Extra Insight" in margin below).

Read Acts 4:13 in the margin, and summarize it in your own words below:

Jesus prefers to fulfill His mission by partnering with ordinary men and women who are simply willing to say yes. If you've ever questioned whether you possess the skills needed to make a difference for God's kingdom, we can put that doubt to rest today. Jesus allows ordinary men and women to do extraordinary things when they trust in His authority over their lives.

2. The shallow end is for those who aren't ready or able to swim; the deep end is for disciples.

When I was a little girl, I was content to splash around in the kiddie pool, unaware of both the adventure and the dangers that awaited in the big pool. As I got older, I learned to venture into the deep end. With it came great challenges but also great rewards for someone who loved to swim. The Christian faith is no different. Jesus calls His disciples into the deep end.

Where does Jesus direct Simon Peter to go in Luke 5:4?

Can you recall a time when Jesus led you into a situation that felt like it was over your head or out of your comfort zone? If so, describe it here.

Extra Insight

"The tradition from the earliest days of the church has been that Luke, a companion of the apostle Paul, wrote both Luke and Acts"[3] (see Luke 1:1-4; Acts 1:13; Colossians 4:14; and 2 Timothy 4:11).

Maybe you're in that kind of season now. Maybe Jesus has thrust you into the impossible and, from your point of view, nothing makes sense. What you need to know is that from Jesus' point of view, you're exactly where you need to be. Simon Peter had dabbled in the shallow end. He had met Jesus previously when his brother Andrew introduced them, but it wasn't until Jesus called him into the deep waters that Jesus invited him to be a disciple. Disciples of Jesus learn to swim when they are in over their heads even when the deep waters are intimidating. Just like Peter, there will come a time when we have to venture out of the shallow end if we want to remain obedient to Jesus.

3. The only qualification for being a disciple is the willingness to say yes.

Sometimes the hardest thing we'll ever do in our walk with Christ is resist the temptation to say no. In those moments, we'll be wise to remember that there is good news on the other side of our yes.

How does Peter respond to Jesus in Luke 5:5?

How willing are you to say yes to Jesus when He calls you into the impossible? Explain your response.

At first, Simon Peter expresses disbelief at Jesus' request. He is an expert fisherman. He spent all night searching for fish in prime conditions, and his nets came up empty. He knows it will be virtually impossible to find fish in the deep waters in the middle of the day.

But there is a *but*: "But because you say so..." Even though it doesn't make sense, Simon Peter is willing to say yes anyway. There is a miracle waiting in the deep waters, and Simon Peter has to determine to obey Jesus before He is allowed to see it.

Like me, you may identify well with Peter's response even after witnessing the miracle of the abundant yield of fish. He replies in verse 8, "Go away from me, Lord; I am a sinful man!" Yet even when we are astonished and humbled over Jesus' power and grace in our lives, He calls us still to simply say, "Yes, Lord, I will follow you."

4. The path of discipleship always involves the invitation of others.

As both an introvert and an independent worker, I confess that involving others is often a struggle for me. But Jesus knows that each of us is better together.

Read Luke 5:9-11. Who else is called to be a disciple on this occasion?

Do you find it easier to obey God alone or in the community of others? Why?

Simon Peter and his two partners, James and John, say goodbye to their job as catchers of fish and hello to their job as catchers of people. Jesus would go on to invite twelve total disciples to join His mission, whom He would teach and encourage to share God's love with the world. You'll recall from our study of Luke 4 that the devil attacked Jesus when He was alone. The application for each of us is that the community of God is always stronger than the isolated follower.

5. Discipleship requires sacrifice.

Sacrifice: this is the part of discipleship that no one likes to talk about. In reality, however, this component of discipleship holds just as much importance as the other four truths we have considered together.

Describe the new disciples' actions in Luke 5:11.

Has Jesus ever asked you to give up something important to you? Explain your response.

These words in the latter half of Luke 5:11 make it sound so easy: They "left everything and followed him." But you and I both know that surrender can be painful. I get cranky when I can't have my coffee in the morning. I don't give things up easily. So, I'm imagining these three new disciples grasping their beloved fishing nets one last time with clinging fingers—one last hesitant glance at the shore that held childhood memories. I could be wrong. But my own experience tells me different. Human hearts are conditioned to hold on to what we think we have.

Jesus' response to His new followers still applies to us today: "Don't be afraid; from now on you will fish for people" (v. 10b). In other words, "I'll equip you for this calling. I'll keep you safe in the deep waters. I'll give you miracles in response to your yes. I'll surround you with community. And I'll be everything you need."

One commentator writes, "Simon, Andrew, James, and John didn't allow the greatest day of their fishing careers to distract them. That day, they determined to follow Jesus anywhere He led and to do anything He commanded. Even if it led them into deeper waters."[4]

Whatever your deep waters look like today, sister, square your shoulders and lift your chin toward the heavens. Jesus is calling you further into His calling for discipleship and He promises to keep you steady as you move forward.

Finding Your Collective

The most stunning truth about Jesus' commitment to discipleship is that He doesn't need us to help Him fulfill His mission. He is perfect and holy, capable of delivering both judgment and grace at any moment to a world that is helpless without Him; yet in love and grace He extends an invitation to join Him in an assignment that will ultimately determine the landscape of eternity.

I think this is why, as we've seen, Peter responds to Jesus' miracle with the deepest expression of humility, essentially saying, "I am not worthy of this calling, Lord." These are words that I whisper often. The sum of my sins would overflow the entire Sea of Galilee. So strong is my capacity for self-destruction that I cannot fathom why Jesus would choose me as His partner. And still He whispers, "Do not be afraid." He whispers the same to you today.

The Bible is the story of God fulfilling His mission through human hands. There's something waiting for you that God needs you to see. There's someone He needs you to love on. There's change brewing that He has set in motion, and He wants you to carry it through. And although He doesn't need us to accomplish His plan—He will see it to completion whether we're on board or not—He longs for us to partner with Him to bring hope into the world. And we do this by partnering with others. God intends for the real work of His kingdom to be done in the collective.

Jesus will tell His disciples later, "The harvest is plentiful, but the workers are few" (Luke 10:2). Our "determined living" job is to find the workers.

In what ways are you already collaborating with others to serve Jesus in your church, community, or world?

Close today by writing the names of three people you could invite to meet you for coffee or lunch to discuss a new way you might partner together to love the world around you. Spend some time praying over these names, asking Jesus to burden their hearts for discipleship as well.

1.

2.

3.

Oh, how I wish I could hear your future report of how Jesus is going to move! Because one thing we can count on: He will make a miracle out of our yes.

Extra Insight

"Just as Jesus is now summoning Simon to follow him, so Simon in turn will bring others to share in the blessings of salvation. Catching fish is a skill requiring training, experience, and patience, and so is evangelism."[5]

—R. T. France

God intends for the real work of His kingdom to be done in the collective.

DAY 3: A FRIEND OF SINNERS

I'm fascinated by stories of the saints who have gone before us and given their lives to serving others in the name of Jesus. R. T. France recalls the story of a young Catholic priest from Belgium who ventured to the Hawaiian island of Molokai. Its luscious green cliffs descending into crystal sparkling waters belied the hidden threat there. Father Damien was on a mission to serve a medically quarantined population that suffered from leprosy. At the age of forty-nine, he would succumb to the disease himself, having contracted it from the very people he came to serve.[1]

What prompts us to actively pursue those who don't fit the popular mold of acceptability? What inspires the choice to engage the misfits, untouchables, unwanted, and unaccepted? It isn't a passionately persuaded opinion or a fleeting feeling that washes over us and then disappears. It's a living Lord, who both comforts and convicts. When we come face-to-face with our need for His mercy, we'll be hungry for the rest of the world to receive it too.

Read Luke 5:27-32, and put a placeholder there for future reference.

The Quick Three
What happened?
Where did it happen?
What characters are mentioned in this reading?

Setting the Scene

Today we meet another disciple who left everything behind for Jesus. Unlike our fishermen from yesterday's reading, Levi was a tax collector. He wasn't just any tax collector, though. One commentator notes that Luke uses the Greek term *telōnēs* to describe Levi, which implies that he was rather corrupt in his business dealings. Levi was a descendant of the Israelite tribe of Levi, which included the Levites who had been designated as priests by God. Instead, Levi likely used his divine inheritance to benefit the Roman Empire. He was considered a traitor among his own people because he served the Gentile nation rather than the Jewish one.[2] We've already seen what the Jewish people thought of the Gentiles in our study of Luke 4.

Now is also a good time to introduce the Pharisees. As one source explains, the Pharisees were a prominent religious group known and admired for their piety. They knew God's law well and were committed to following it to the letter. Unfortunately, they didn't embrace the gift of grace that Jesus taught, and they expected others to live by standards that they could not meet themselves.[3] We often hear the Pharisees described as hypocritical, and we're about to find out why.

A Party-Goer and a Party-Thrower

My friends and acquaintances are among my richest blessings in life, and I'm sure you would say the same. I share similar experiences, backgrounds, beliefs, and life circumstances with many of them. Our common bonds and connections make life and our times together infinitely sweeter. But I am also fortunate to have friends and acquaintances with whom I have virtually nothing or very little in common, and I enjoy getting together with them too. Because of our distinct differences, they challenge the way that I think and respond to the world around me. Yet regardless of our similarities or differences, one thing remains the same: we all are in need of a Savior. It's true today, and it was true in Jesus' day too.

According to Luke 5:29, who does Levi invite to his party?

Based on what you know now about Levi as a tax collector, do you think his guests would have been described as corrupt or not? Why?

A corrupt tax collector meets the Savior of the world and decides to leave everything behind to follow Him. He's so excited about this life-changing moment that he invites his best friends and colleagues to eat, drink, and celebrate with him so they can meet this man called Jesus. Although Jesus, Levi, and his friends are having a grand time at this party, there is a group of people who are most decidedly not. As one source points out, "Most blocks in Capernaum consisted of four homes facing a common courtyard."[4] Not having been invited to the party, the Pharisees were probably standing in or near the courtyard backing up to Levi's home as they grumbled to Jesus' disciples.

What did the Pharisees ask about Jesus in verse 30?

Extra Insight

You may recognize Levi better by the name of Matthew. His story is also recorded in Matthew 9:9-13.

Extra Insight

Jesus did much of His ministry around the dinner table, and this action is particularly prominent in Luke. You can also see Him sharing meals with others in these verses in Luke's Gospel: 7:36-50; 9:10-17; 10:38-42; 11:37-54; 14:1-24; 19:1-10; 22:7-39; 24:28-32; and 24:36-43.

Can you recall a time when you have been asked a similar question? Why are you spending time with *that girl*? Why did you invite *them* to our dinner? Why are you sitting next to *that family* at church?

If so, congratulations. You've lived like Jesus. But maybe you've been that girl. Maybe you are that family. Maybe you don't look like the members on the front row at church. Maybe you don't feel comfortable going to church at all. Maybe you've made some mistakes that are difficult for those around you to forget. Hear this clearly today: you are welcome in the body of Christ. Jesus longs to dine with you.

How does Jesus respond in Luke 5:31?

Perhaps Luke chuckled as he was writing Jesus' words. As a physician himself, he would have understood well the analogy Jesus was making. Jesus didn't come to heal the perfect. He came to save the sick. But if you're sensing a bit of irony in Jesus' statement, you would be correct. There is no one who is perfect. I can imagine Him saying these words to the Pharisees with a corner of His mouth upturned, wondering if they would realize the hypocrisy reflected in their question.

How were the Pharisees any different from Levi and his dinner party guests? They weren't. And Jesus called them out on it. The problem was, they refused to acknowledge that they, too, were sinners in need of grace.

8 It is by grace you have been saved, through faith—and this is not from yourselves, it is the gift of God—9 not by works, so that no one can boast.

(Ephesians 2:8-9)

Read Ephesians 2:8-9 in the margin. What do these verses tell us about our salvation?

Now read Romans 3:10 in the margin. How do you think the Pharisees would have responded to these words?

As it is written: "There is no one righteous, not even one."

(Romans 3:10)

How do you respond to this truth?

Does it surprise you that of all the places Jesus could be on this particular night, he chose to dine with sinners? Why or why not?

Consider your own friends and acquaintances. This may not be a question that you can answer fully because only Jesus knows our hearts, but how many of your friends and acquaintances do not know Him? Or, to think about this question another way, are the majority of your interactions with fellow believers or do you seek out unbelievers as well? Rather than accept the culture's attitude toward groups and classes of people, Jesus loved all people equally. He intentionally pursued those who were seen as "less than" within society. We will be wise to remember how easy it is for us to fall into the same mind-set that the Pharisees possessed and, instead, seek to embrace Jesus' attitude toward all.

If we have trouble relating in our own lives with those who do not know Jesus, perhaps we need to remind ourselves how Jesus viewed them and responded to their repentance. Though we will study Luke 15 later, for now let's look at a few verses in this chapter about a lost sheep, a lost coin, and a lost son.

Turn to Luke 15, and read verses 6, 9, and 23. What clues do we find in these verses about Jesus' attitude and emotions toward those who find salvation in Him?

Have you ever considered that this is how Jesus feels when you make the decision to place your faith and trust in Him?

Let this be a reminder today: Jesus is a party-thrower and a party-goer. He celebrates everyone who comes to repentance, including us. What's more, He intentionally seeks out those who need Him.

There are four things we can observe about Jesus today:

1. He deliberately pursued those in need of grace and mercy.
2. He hung out where they did. He didn't expect them to come to Him.
3. He met their physical needs first by sharing meals and breaking bread together, with the intent of meeting their spiritual needs when they recognized Him as their Savior as Levi did.
4. He invites celebration and joy, rather than legalism and restraint.

Are you following Jesus' example by choosing to intentionally engage with those who do not know Him? If so, how? And if not, why?

Befriending the World

If befriending the world seems overwhelming, there are two simple steps we can take today.

Step 1: *Recognize our own need for Jesus' forgiveness.*

It's easy to peer down our noses at the Pharisees as they refused to recognize their own sinful nature. Let's determine not to do the same. We are all sinners. We all need Jesus. The sun will not set on a day when we won't have a need for repentance.

However, the beauty of repentance is that it is a privileged gift. Think back to when you were young and had made a mistake. I once stole a piece of gum from the local convenience store when I was seven. Not wanting to tell my mom what I had done, I put it off until I could no longer hide the shame on my face. Had I known what her response would have been, I wouldn't have waited so long to tell her that I was sorry for my misstep. Of course, there was a consequence. I had to return the piece of gum (which, thankfully for the store clerk's sake, was unused) and apologize in person to the store owner. I'm sure I also lost the freedom of playing with my favorite toy or some such other punishment that I have long since forgotten.

But immediately after the consequence, there was grace. My mother beautifully emulated how Jesus responds to our sin every single day. With repentance comes swift forgiveness.

Maybe you have a similar story, or maybe you don't. Maybe you acknowledged your mistake and your consequence came with harsh punishment without any grace. Despite our human experiences, we can rejoice that we have the privilege of repentance with a Holy Savior. We serve a God who celebrates when we say *I'm sorry*.

Is there something you need to seek forgiveness for today from God and others? Go ahead and write a plan below that you can act on today or in the near future.

Step 2: Find a way to engage or serve those who do not know Jesus.

There is a difference between run-in coincidences with unbelievers and the deliberate pursuit of their hearts by sharing the love of Jesus. We need to prioritize the latter. Having a five-minute conversation with my neighbor that I see in the grocery doesn't qualify as living like Jesus. A key indicator of how well we are emulating Him is the amount of time we spend pursuing and serving those who do not know Him.

Here are a few tips for engaging with those who do not know Jesus:

- Invite a friend to join you. This is why Jesus calls us to discipleship. His work is easier when we do it together.
- Fill others' physical needs first. Feed them. Invite them into your home. Help them decorate their house. Assist them in a task at work. Look for unmet needs, and then follow through to help fill them.
- Be creative. Hang out where they hang out. This probably won't be at the fellowship meal at church (not that there's anything wrong with that...I'll see you there for fried chicken). Think outside the box of your usual hangouts, and go to where they are.
- Lead with prayer. Dr. John Ewart, an interim pastor at my home church, always taught that the majority of individuals respond positively to prayer. Even if they don't yet understand who Jesus is, they will probably understand the concept of prayer and are likely to welcome your offer to pray with them.
- Be prepared to receive criticism in response to creatively reaching out to those not in the church. This is a hard reality, but one we need to brace ourselves for. There will always be a Pharisee in our midst. Let's pray it isn't us!

If you love people well, you won't ever have to defend your faith. Look someone in the eye with kindness today. Go out of your way to love someone who doesn't look like you, think like you, talk like you, or believe like you. That last one might stir up some Pharisaical conversation, but I think Jesus would wholeheartedly approve.

Spread the love of Jesus around like you've got too much of it to keep for yourself. Don't worry; there's a never-ending supply. Jesus, *give us wisdom and courage to live like You!*

Close today by praying over these questions.

- Who can I call on to help me intentionally engage the community around me?
- What physical needs can I fill today for someone who does not
- know Jesus?
- Where can I go that might introduce me to a different circle of friends?

A key indicator of how well we are emulating Jesus is the amount of time we spend pursuing and serving those who do not know Him.

DAY 4: THE UPSIDE-DOWN KINGDOM

One of the quickest ways for the enemy to distract me from determined living is to get me to focus on my circumstances instead of my faith. I think you and I can agree that we are all juggling more things than we ought to be. It's how we humans roll. Too many things to juggle, too many distractions, too little time. We waste neurons focusing on the wrong things, and we become panicky instead of peaceful.

Then a giant surprise hits us in the face, and we're struggling to catch our breath. The phone call from the doctor. The layoff that comes out of the blue. The betrayal of a trusted friend. Where is Jesus in those moments? Can we still say that life is good when life around us most certainly is *not good*?

Our Master Teacher is about to deliver a master class on the true call of discipleship. Here's the short version: our circumstances don't have jurisdiction over our attitude, and following Jesus will help us see things with the right perspective. When our world is turned upside down, He is our level place.

We can take back our peace today by giving Him space to work.

Read Luke 6:12-26, and put a placeholder there for future reference.

The Quick Three
What happened?
Where did it happen?
What characters are mentioned in this reading?

Setting the Scene

Earlier this week, we introduced discipleship as the foundation of Jesus' ministry. Today we will see Him use that to deliver the backbone of His teachings. From the top of the mountain after a night of prayer, Jesus descends to officially choose and then coach His disciples on the conditions of following Him.

But Jesus is surrounded by more than just His chosen Twelve. A large crowd has gathered along the Sea of Galilee—some to hear His teachings, some to be healed. All of them would be changed forever if they took His message to heart.

We've seen previously that discipleship requires sacrifice. Jesus is about to tell us why it's worth it.

The Blessed Ones

Would you describe your life as blessed? Why or why not?

The twenty-first century has done little to help us understand the biblical concept of blessing. Saying that someone is blessed in today's culture usually implies one or more of the following conditions: financial prosperity, a fortunate lifestyle, or sheer luck. The term is so overused that in some circles it can even be interpreted with sarcasm.

Rarely does the word *blessed* convey the biblical definition of the word. Let's discover it together.

Read Luke 6:20-22. How many times in these verses does Jesus define *blessing*?

Extra Insight

If you find that the flow of Jesus' teaching in Luke 6 is a little halted, it's probably due to the fact that this is not a literal transcription of His sermon. Luke "gave us a concentrated sampling of this teaching time."[1]

One commentary explains that the transliteration of the word *blessed* in this passage is the Greek word *makarios*. Here it means to be a "recipient of divine favor."[2] Greek readers of Luke's Gospel would have recognized this word and variations of it from Mary's song of praise in Luke 1.

Read Luke 1:46-55, and describe in your own words how Mary described what it meant to be *blessed*:

Mary's definition of blessed relied on which of the following? Circle all that apply:

what God had done for her   her circumstances in life

how people would view her   quality traits God had given her

the character of God   her beauty

how God had helped His people   how much money she had

God's faithfulness

Extra Insight

As one source points out, scholars disagree as to whether Jesus' sermon from the level place in Luke 6 is the same as the Sermon on the Mount found in Matthew 5–7. They could be two different events or Luke's version might be a shorter retelling of Matthew's more comprehensive one.[3]

Can you relate to Mary's understanding? How has your life been blessed in these ways?

Here in Luke 6, Jesus is teaching about what it means to be blessed. I find it amusing how verse 17 notes that Jesus teaches from "a level place." It's amusing because what Jesus is proposing turns the notion of the kingdom of God upside down. But let's pause for a moment to make sure we don't miss this truth: whatever you are facing today, Jesus is your level place. We can rejoice even if things around us don't make sense because He always stands steady and ready to see us through.

From His level place, Jesus reminds His disciples that our circumstances don't have jurisdiction over our attitudes when we remember His perspective. The presence of blessing is defined by our faith in God's reality, not our own.

Review Luke 6:20-23 and complete the chart below:

You are blessed when you are...	In what way will God see to your blessing?	Describe a time when you felt this way.	Describe how Jesus responded to you then.
Poor			
Hungry			
Sorrowful			
Persecuted			

Sister, this is radical. I'm willing to bet that no one you know would use the word *blessed* when referring to poverty, hunger, sorrow, or persecution—unless, of course, they know Jesus.

What does Jesus promise in John 10:10?

Does Jesus' teaching on the blessed life align with your definition of abundant life? Why or why not?

R. T. France writes of this passage, "There are only two responses to Jesus' message, either wholehearted commitment to the kingdom of God, with all the hardships that may bring, or continued pursuit of the way of the world, putting present satisfaction before the will of God and its ultimate rewards."[4]

Whether we realize it or not, we will determine to choose one of these options. If we give our circumstances a voice, we'll choose the wrong one. Like Mary, we must be wholeheartedly committed to the kingdom of God. To do that, we'll have to determine to hear Jesus' voice above all others.

Jesus Sees You . . . and the World

"What happens when we have another medical event?" I asked my husband.

"We'll cross that bridge when we get to it, and we'll be ready," he replied.

We crossed that bridge the week of an approaching magazine deadline in which I was to share my story. That afternoon brought some unusual abdominal pain and a nine-hour stay at the ER. With two known aneurysms and a vEDS diagnosis, that kind of pain isn't something you mess around with. After several tests, we still didn't have a definitive source for my unusual abdominal pain; but we knew that it wasn't immediately life-threatening. It seemed that this was just a baby bump in the road, and for that we are grateful.

For the magazine article, I had agreed to tell how God has redeemed my story and turned something bad into something good. Hear me clearly on this: He has done that. Praising God's faithfulness and redemptive love will always be my story. But the very raw truth hidden in my emotions on any given day is that I do not want this to be my story. I'd like another one, please. One that isn't filled with scary unknowns and uncertainties. Most mornings my circumstances make me want to hibernate. But instead I put two feet on the floor, because Jesus sees me and calls me blessed.

This is your story too.

- When you long for your financial situation to even out, Jesus sees you and calls you blessed.
- When you thirst for the presence of Jesus in the bleakest of moments, Jesus sees you and calls you blessed.

- When you cry yourself to sleep at night, Jesus sees you and calls you blessed.
- When you are rejected and even made fun of because of your faith, Jesus sees you and calls you blessed.

I want you to see something that always makes me stop and read this passage again. Jesus' use of a personal pronoun here is not an accident. He does so to emphasize His tenderness toward you.

Reread Luke 6:20-23 below. I have altered it slightly so that we can make it as personal as Jesus intended it. Fill in each blank with your name, and then read it aloud:

Looking at _____, he said:

"Blessed is _____ when she is poor,
for hers is the kingdom of God.

Blessed is _____ when she hungers,
for she will be satisfied.

Blessed is _____ when she weeps,
for she will laugh.

Blessed is _____ when people hate her,
    when they exclude her and insult her
    and reject her name as evil,
        because of the Son of Man.

"Rejoice in that day and leap for joy, because great is your reward in heaven. For that is how their ancestors treated the prophets.
                        (Luke 6:20-23, author's paraphrase)

Sister, it is critical that you and I determine to hear Jesus' voice over us when our circumstances are challenging. We'll remember that Jesus' purpose in making disciples is to carry the love of God throughout the entire earth.

One commentator notes that when Jesus was here on earth, the world held an estimated three hundred million people, while today it holds over five billion.[5] The challenge for us today to deliver the love of Christ to all nations is almost incomprehensible, but certainly not impossible when relying on the strength of heaven.

When we are hit by that giant surprise, what would happen if we chose to hear Jesus' voice instead of the world's? When life around us is *definitely not good*, what would happen if we would rise and say anyway, "My Lord calls me blessed"?

Would that be radical? Absolutely. The kingdom of God is as upside down and radical as you can imagine. But Jesus says that is what it will take for God's glory to take over the world. Radically different from anything we know, those who embrace Jesus' upside-down kingdom are radically productive toward building the kingdom of God.

I know it won't be an easy task, but it can be done by desperately clinging to Jesus and determining to hear His voice. Tomorrow we'll dig deeper into how Jesus wants us to build the kingdom of God. But today, rest in the knowledge that you are blessed, beloved. Jesus says so.

DAY 5: REFLECTIVE LOVE

There is a coursing undercurrent running beneath the teachings of Jesus declaring that the expectations of His followers should be different from those of the world. Watch only the surface of His river of truth, and it's a beautiful story that changed everything. One that could change you, if you let it. But dip your toe into those flooding waters of truth, and you'll find that to live like Jesus means to deny the world.

Today it means to deny the self. But what does that mean—especially in a culture that encourages *self*-care?

Self-care generally means finding ways to holistically tend to the health of your mind, body, and soul, and let me clarify that I'm not bashing that. Jesus demonstrated the need for balance and renewal, as we saw on Day 1 this week. But I think the most authentic expression of self-care is Sabbath rest—which actually turns our focus toward God and community. That is what I prefer to call soul-care, and it's always a good thing. In fact, it's a needed thing. God modeled this for us on the seventh day of the Creation story and commanded us to observe it weekly.

Though there certainly is a time for self-care or soul-care, followers of Jesus *are* called to a higher standard of putting others' needs before our own as He did. The good news, however, is that the higher standard brings a greater spiritual reward of making us more like Jesus. And this world absolutely needs more of *that*.

Read Luke 6:27-36, and put a placeholder there for future reference.

The Quick Three
What happened?
Where did it happen?

Radically different from anything we know, those who embrace Jesus' upside-down kingdom are radically productive toward building the kingdom of God.

Setting the Scene

Yesterday we saw how radical the kingdom of God is. Today as Jesus continues His sermon to His disciples, He takes us deeper into that mentality. If yesterday's teaching was radical, today's is downright unfathomable.

Jesus' Jewish listeners would have been familiar with the divine command to love your neighbor as yourself. They would have remembered its reverent echo from Leviticus: "Do not seek revenge or bear a grudge against anyone among your people, but love your neighbor as yourself. I am the Lord" (Leviticus 19:18).

But Jesus went further, saying we are to love our *enemies*. I can imagine quite a few hands being raised as these words spilled from His mouth. Or maybe they just skipped the raised hands altogether and went straight to jaw dropping. We humans are naturally predisposed to dislike our enemies. What Jesus was asking was unheard of.

Although some of the examples Jesus offers might seem foreign to us today, the principles still apply. Enemies abound, but Jesus wants to change the way we treat them.

And deeper we go into the rules of the upside-down kingdom...

An Alternative Society

One of the hardest things I've ever had to come to terms with is the fact that we will have unpleasant experiences with people who don't like us. Both a people-pleaser and a conflict avoider by nature, I get uneasy when I am rejected, insulted, or wrongly perceived.

What is your gut reaction when people treat you poorly?

Enemy is a strong word and one I do not use often. But God's Word tells us that anyone who endeavors to live like Christ will develop enemies (2 Timothy 3:12). *Strong's Concordance* tells us that the transliteration of the Greek word for enemy in today's reading is *echthros*, meaning "someone *openly hostile* . . . [or] animated by a *deep-seated* hatred," and that can imply "irreconcilable hostility, proceeding out of a personal hatred bent on inflicting harm."[1]

Using this biblical definition of an enemy, can you recall an exchange or a relationship with someone who exhibited this behavior? If so, describe it here:

When Jesus said we are to love our enemies, He was calling us to *agape* love. One commentary explains that *agape* is the Greek word that means love, but it doesn't refer to the romantic love between a man and a woman, nor the brotherly love found between two friends. It describes agape love as "a distinctly Christian kind of love that seeks the greatest good of another."[2] It is unconditional, benevolent, and rare. This is the type of love Jesus intended, and this is the type of love He modeled.

We see agape love in Jesus' determined mission to save us from sin and death. And we can look to Scripture to give us specific examples of how He displayed this selfless love.

Extra Insight

Paul eloquently defines agape love in 1 Corinthians 13.

Look up the passages below, and note beside each how Jesus exemplified selfless love:

Mark 10:45

2 Corinthians 8:9

Philippians 2:5-8

Reread Luke 6:27, and then consider what we know lies ahead for Jesus in Jerusalem (Matthew 16:21). What is one of the most profound ways in which Jesus fulfilled the instruction to love our enemies?

Now, let's unpack Jesus' imperative to love our enemies.

Refer to Luke 6:27-31, and fill in the missing words below:

_____ your enemies.

_____ good to those who hate you.

_____ those who curse you.

_____ for those who mistreat you.

If someone slaps you on one cheek, _____ to them the other also.

If someone takes your coat, _____ _____ _____
your shirt from them.

_____ to everyone who asks you.

If anyone takes what belongs to you, _____ _____
_____ it back.

_____ unto others as you would have them do unto you.

Grammatically, what do each of the underlined words have in common?

Not one of these commands is written with a passive verb. Each of them is written with an active verb. It won't be enough to live and let live when someone is hostile. It won't be enough to silently move on when you are wronged. Living like Jesus by loving our enemies requires *action*.

Think carefully about the ways in which someone may have treated you with deep-seated hatred. What about someone who acted upon a specific intent to cause harm? Take a moment to pray over the incidences that come to mind.

Now write a simple way you can obey each command below by responding with selfless love. You may or may not want to personalize it with a particular person's name.

Jesus' Command	My Response
Love your enemies.	I will . . .
Do good to those who hate you.	I will . . .
Bless those who curse you.	I will . . .
Pray for those who mistreat you.	I will . . .

If someone slaps you on one cheek, turn to them the other also.	I will …
If someone takes your coat, do not withhold your shirt from them.	I will …
Give to everyone who asks you	I will …
If anyone takes what belongs to you, do not demand it back.	I will …
Do unto others as you would have them do unto you.	I will …

Be merciful, just as your Father is merciful. (Luke 6:36)

Can I be perfectly candid with you? This is hard. My fleshly response to those who have wronged me is to retreat, not to pursue with love. But Jesus makes it clear that the expectation for His disciples is that we would actively love the unlovable.

It's likely that you have someone in your life right now who is difficult to love. Let's consider this very real dilemma for a moment: what do we do when we cannot love someone? How do we respond to the unlovable? Understanding Jesus' commands to love our enemies is one thing, but following through may produce a hurdle that we cannot jump over on our own. Loving our enemies requires heavenly help. As daughters of a merciful Savior who understands every feeling we will ever experience, we can ask for help in every situation.

Read the passages in the margin, and record what each tells us about the work of the Holy Spirit:

Romans 5:5

Galatians 5:22-23

Jesus does not expect us to do this work on our own. When we are faced with the difficult task of loving our enemies, we can call on the strength of heaven to help us.

Extra Insight

Scholars make it clear that Jesus was not advocating for the acceptance or promotion of criminal violence, abuse, or mistreatment at the hands of an offender. As one writer notes, "He wasn't calling His disciples to become the world's punching bag."[3] When you consider the holistic view of Jesus' ministry, it is clear that He defends the victim in such situations, always.

Hope does not put us to shame, because God's love has been poured out into our hearts through the Holy Spirit, who has been given to us.
(Romans 5:5)

[22]The fruit of the Spirit is love, joy, peace, forbearance, kindness, goodness, faithfulness, [23]gentleness and self-control. Against such things there is no law.
(Galatians 5:22-23)

Consider these words of R. T. France:

Discipleship is a process of growing into the family likeness. However, this is to be achieved not merely by adopting a new set of behavioral rules but also by absorbing God's own values and attitudes. This means, above all, an outgoing, uncalculating love that puts the needs and interests of others before our own. A community that lives by such principles will stand out against natural human self-centeredness as an alternative society, incomprehensible perhaps, but undeniably attractive.[4]

How can loving our enemies benefit both others and ourselves?

Our Choices Matter

If we want to truly live like Jesus, we'll have to pursue our enemies with agape love—selfless, unconditional, forgiving, and relentless love. Our determination to seek their best interest will show them that Jesus' alternative society is one worth embracing. It will keep our perspective on what matters most: the power of Jesus in us to bring healing to a broken world. And it will repeatedly beat down the fleshly desire rising up to announce that our lives hold more value than anyone else's. Responding to hostility with love will help us embrace Jesus' selfless posture.

We had dinner with our extended family recently. My niece and nephew are five and four, respectively. To say that they adore my eleven-year-old son, Thomas, would be an understatement. They watch everything he does, try to emulate his behavior, and desire nothing more than to be near him when we are together. Watching these sweet cousins grow up together is one of the greatest blessings of my life.

Before dinner we reminded Thomas that his behavior choices matter. The way he treats the people around him matters, not just because we asked him to be kind and respectful but also because others would be watching. His younger cousins would emulate his behavior whether it was polite or not.

The same is true when we love our enemies. Our actions are on display. People are watching. Do we want them to see fleshly, selfish behavior, or do we want them to see Jesus? How is the world to know God's love if we do not reflect it ourselves?

Let's close today by putting Jesus' teachings into practice by spending some dedicated time in prayer over those we consider enemies. Ask the Holy Spirit for strength to love them. Ask for God's favor over their lives. And wait expectantly for Jesus to renew your Spirit as you walk closely with Him in loving the world.

Extra Insight

"In the Old Testament, prophets and poets wisely rested in the promise that God would take just vengeance on their behalf (e.g., Deut. 32:35; Ps. 94:1).

"Jesus took this a step further. He not only expected His disciples to leave vengeance in the hands of God, He also called for them to petition the Lord for mercy on the people who cause harm!"
—Charles Swindoll[5]

Luke 6:43-45.

The way we live is determined by what occupies our _____.

Philippians 4:8

Filling our hearts and minds with the _____ of God ensures that the overflow of our actions will be for God's good.

Storing up God's good in our hearts releases us from the pressure of having to _____ it all.

Week 3

The Rescuer

Determined to Save Humankind

(Luke 7–9)

> 4What is man that you are mindful of him,
>   and the son of man that you care for him?
>
> 5Yet you have made him a little lower than the
> heavenly beings
>   and crowned him with glory and honor.
>   (Psalm 8:4-5 ESV)

I was standing in the sandy soil on my grandmother's farm when my hair started to fall out. Chatting with my cousin and absentmindedly raking my fingers through my hair, I didn't expect the long, brown chunks that appeared in my fists. My doctor had warned me that hair loss might result from the two twelve-hour surgeries I had recently endured. I just wasn't quite as prepared as I should have been for the sudden loss of it all.

I let the hair slip through my fingers as lighter strands were carried away by the breeze and heavier chunks fell to the ground. I combed my fingers through my hair again and again, and it seemed there was no end to the loss coming from my scalp. Raking and releasing, this is how I let go of the hair that had been with me for years.

My hair wasn't the only thing that had to be released. With the diagnosis that followed the surgeries came the reality that life as I knew it would be markedly different. Limitations within this new reality would abound. With no cure or treatment available for the genetic disorder I now knew I carried, I was forced to let go of dreams I had nurtured for as many years as my hair had grown. A career in the fitness industry, gone. The hope of growing our family with another child, gone. The expectation of living long enough to meet my grandchildren, gone.

With all that had been seemingly lost, it would have been easy to assume that the life I had lived so far had been insignificant to its Creator. It would have been easy to assume that Jesus knew nothing of the hair that was lost, the dreams that were released, and the emptiness that followed.

Except that His Word tells me otherwise.

I've been a follower of Jesus for almost thirty years, and I have to be honest with you: all this time I thought I knew Him. I knew His story. I knew why He came and why He died. I knew why He ascended into heaven and why He promised to return. But I didn't know why He was so determined to love me until I studied the Gospel of Luke.

If you've ever wondered if you matter to the Savior of the world, I hope this week of our study will prove that He carries you in His heart. He knows everything about you, even down to the strands of hair that He counted Himself. He sees every dream that might have been released and every tear that you think goes unnoticed. And He's longing to crown you with the glory that comes from entrusting your heart to His.

DAY 1: RESCUE FROM GRIEF (DETERMINED TO BE COMPASSIONATE)

This might be a grossly simplified statement on public opinion, but it has been my observation that people tend to believe one of two things about the attitude of God toward humanity. Either they believe that He is a kind and benevolent God of grace or that He is a harsh and distant God of punishment. The details of both definitions might vary a little, but most are inclined to pigeonhole God's actions into one of these corners.

For those who lean toward the harsh and distant camp, it might be difficult to view God as sympathetic to the loss and despair we see every day. Just a fifteen-minute snippet of the news will almost always prompt the questions: *Does God care*? *Does He even see us when we are hurting*?

I can understand that. I asked those questions just before I started writing this study. You see, the genetic disorder I live with is often defined as *terminal*. It is life-limiting in that there is a shortened life expectancy attached with the diagnosis. I don't like that word *terminal*. It's not an easy word to carry, even though we all carry it whether we recognize it or not. As I was wondering once again if God is inherently graceful or fundamentally punishing, I asked Him those questions: *God, do you care that I now have to carry this word around as a label*? *Do you see me when that word brings me to tears before I close my eyes at night*?

It was through the passage we are studying today that God tenderly showed me that He does, in fact, care. It was this passage that led me to study the Gospel of Luke, where I realized I was not the first to have walked this earth with the awareness that death was on the way. Jesus carried the *terminal* label around too. But He was determined to obliterate it.

For anyone like me who has wondered if God is a punishing God, this passage from Luke 7 was written for you.

Read Luke 7:11-17, and put a placeholder there for future reference.

The Quick Three
What happened?
Where did it happen?
What characters are mentioned in this reading?

Setting the Scene

Jesus has finished laying out His specific instructions to His disciples and now turns His attention back to active ministry work. This takes Him through Capernaum and to the small town of Nain. One source notes that Nain was about twenty-five miles from Capernaum and, as a small town, was a "relatively insignificant place in Galilee."[1]

Something prompted Jesus to visit this remote area, but we aren't told what. It is highly plausible that what drove Jesus to visit Nain was simply the mysterious and divine will of God. As in life, it isn't unusual to witness biblical occurrences that have no easily recognizable catalyst. There is a unique beauty in this truth, which we'll discover together in a moment.

The scene of Nicodemus preparing Jesus' body for burial in John 19:39-40 paints a detailed picture of what Jesus might have seen as He approached the city gate. The mother's son would have been wrapped in seventy-five pounds of spices and resin to combat the natural decomposing process.

For a widow who had now lost her only son, the reality of her new normal would be devastating. As one commentary points out, there would be no one to provide or care for her any longer, and because Jewish society would see her as a burden rather than a contributing member, she would face constant obstacles in meeting her basic needs.[2] We would expect to see a coffin, but in this setting, it was a bier, which was "a lattice frame supported by horizontal poles" to carry the body to the family's burial place.[3] According to Jewish mourning customs, the mother would have been walking in front of the bier and so would have seen Jesus first.[4]

His Heart Went Out to Her

This scene evokes compassion within us, just as it did for Jesus. If I were to describe compassion in the simplest of terms, I would say that it is noticing someone is hurt and doing whatever it takes to try and fix that hurt.

Would you describe yourself as a compassionate person?
Why or why not?

List several tangible examples of how you might display compassion:

Because I am a visual learner and I'm wondering if maybe you are too,
humor me for a moment. Keeping in mind the information we've learned
about the scene of today's passage, reread the verses again and look for
the details of the story. List them here:

Now, re-create the details visually by drawing the scene below. Remember, I
said to humor me. It's okay; I'll be drawing stick figures too.

Now rewrite Luke 7:13 word for word below:

If you are reading from the ESV, NASB, KJV, or CSB translations, you have
just written that Jesus had compassion on the grieving mother. But I rather
prefer the wording of the NIV translation: "When the Lord saw her, his heart
went out to her and he said, 'Don't cry'" (Luke 7:13).

His *heart went out to her*. What a beautiful sequence of words. When I consider
the scenarios when I might use similar wording to describe my response to
people, I remember moments when I wrapped my arms around a friend who was
crying, gave money to someone in dire need, or determined to fix someone's
urgent problem. When the heart is moved, the mind and body are put in motion.
Compassion prompts action.

What action does Jesus take in response to seeing the mother with
compassion? (v. 14)

Think tenderly about a season of grief in your life. Perhaps it's one you've
walked through previously, or perhaps you are walking through it now.
(I use the word *tenderly* because I know you have such a season. Until

Jesus comes again to defeat death once and for all, the human condition will be stained with sorrow.) During this season of grief, did you view God as a compassionate God? This may be a complicated question, so take your time with the answer.

Why do you think Jesus was compassionate toward this mother?

There are two inferences that come to the surface when reading this passage—one that would be noticeable to the Jewish observers in Nain, and the other that will be noticeable to us.

To identify the first one, read 1 Kings 17:20-23 and note any similarities to our reading in Luke 7:11-17.

You might know that the 1 Kings passage is the story of the Gentile widow retold by Jesus in His hometown synagogue in Nazareth (Luke 4:26). You also might know that this story caused great anger and rejection among Jesus' listeners because they were not happy with a Messiah promising salvation for the entire world. Luke is very deliberate to make sure his readers notice the connection between the two events. The mourners in Nain would have noticed it too.

How do the mourners in Nain respond in Luke 7:16? What do they recognize about God?

The Nain observers recognize that Jesus' miracle was an act of God, and that God sees and responds to His people. What they haven't quite figured out yet is that Jesus *is* God. They only see Him as a prophet at this point.

For the second inference, let's consider that perhaps one of the reasons Jesus' heart goes out to the mother is because He sees her burying her *only son*. I need to be quite honest with you. This is where this passage punches me in the gut. As I consider Jesus walking toward this woman, determined to fulfill His mission to save the world and knowing what is coming, He is moved to heal her only son because He, too, is an only son who is destined to die.

Extra Insight

In writing about Luke 7:11-17, Warren Wiersbe writes, "Two only sons meet. One was alive but destined to die, the other dead but destined to live."[5]

Luke doesn't tell this story with many details, but He doesn't need to. The foreshadowing of the cross creates enough of an echo to leave an impression in our minds. Jesus is motivated by His compassion for the world.

There's nothing in this story that indicates Jesus acts for any reason other than His deep compassion for the broken. He isn't asked to heal. The mother isn't known for her faith. Jesus simply sees her hurting and is moved. It's this same compassion that will send Him to the cross for you and me.

What is your greatest source of grief today?

Lay it down at Jesus' feet now. He sees you and is moved with compassion. Allow Him to dry your tears. There is always hope in a Savior determined to heal our hurts.

A God of Compassion

I hope what we are studying today is bringing you much hope and comfort. I hope it has convinced or reminded you that God is indeed a kind, benevolent, and compassionate God. I hope Jesus' tender words "Do not weep" (v. 13 NASB) have soothed the weariest of places in your heart. First and foremost, these are the things I am praying over you today.

But it's not enough.

Walk with the wise and become wise, for a companion of fools suffers harm.
(Proverbs 13:20)

Read Proverbs 13:20 in the margin. What advice does this verse give us about the friends we choose?

Proverbs 13:20 gives us sage advice: we become like the company we keep. Perhaps this is why I adore spending time with one of my dearest friends, Kristen. Her gift is compassion. Mine is not. I tend to be more of a "put your big girl panties on and deal with it" kind of friend, while Kristen immediately sees the heart of one who is heartbroken and is moved to show compassion.

I want to be more like Kristen, because she emulates the Jesus of Luke 7 so well. I want to be more like her because I know the world sees God's love through her. I want to be more compassionate because it's what Jesus commands of me. Maybe you do too. By acting with compassion toward those around us, we can help the world recognize God's tender love for humanity.

Read the following verses. Choose one to rewrite in your own words on the following page:

Ephesians 4:32   **Colossians 3:12-13**   **Galatians 6:2**

My paraphrase:

Is there someone in your life who needs compassion today? If so, write their name here, and then spend a few minutes in prayer for them.

Now, brainstorm some tangible ways to show them compassion. (If you don't think your heart is going out to them enough, ask Jesus to give you a greater burden for their needs.)

Finally, make a plan to follow through on one of the things you wrote above. Write any notes below:

By acting with compassion toward those around us, we can help the world recognize God's tender love for humanity.

Don't hesitate; just move. Do it today. If today is coming to a close, put it in your calendar, and see to it that it's done tomorrow. There are people around you who are questioning if God is a God of grace or a God of punishment. Let's show them that He is a God of compassion.

DAY 2: RESCUE FROM SIN (DETERMINED TO BE DEVOTED)

If I only have this one week of freedom, it will be enough.

I whispered these words to Jesus many years ago after repenting from a particular sin. The consequences of that sin had taken its toll on the front end, bringing desperation, unhappiness, and sorrow. So tangled was my mind with lies that I assumed the consequences would linger even though I had sought His forgiveness.

I was wrong.

Jesus' grace was swift, and He was quick to renew my soul. But because I was still naively accustomed to expecting human reactions from a heavenly Father, I kept waiting for the catch. I assumed there would be a caveat, something to negate His forgiveness and label me as unworthy of His love.

I was wrong.

One week of freedom turned into two. Weeks turned into months and then years and I'm still praising His faithfulness and mercy. There are many things that keep me clinging to God's Word, but it's that one week after my repentance that keeps me clinging to Jesus. His tenderness and mercy over my fractured soul sparked an allegiance that I refuse to break. He is the constant pursuer of my heart, and I am simply the recipient of His unfathomable grace.

When you come face-to-face with a Savior determined to love, you don't want any other way.

Read Luke 7:36-50, and put a placeholder there for future reference.

The Quick Three
What happened?
Where did it happen?
What characters are mentioned in this reading?

Setting the Scene

If you threw a dinner party tonight, inviting your dearest family and friends, it would look quite different from the one set before us in Luke 7. There would be a table and food, and surely discussion would ensue, but that's where most of the similarities would end.

Luke doesn't tell us why Simon the Pharisee invited Jesus to His party. Swindoll notes that it was likely "the Pharisee was simply curious or perhaps trying to appear magnanimous by hosting a political or religious rival."[1] Whatever the reason, Jesus went. Pharisees needed a Savior too.

Another commentator notes that guests dined by reclining on the floor around a central table: "Banquet participants would lay on their left side, so they could eat with their right hand, with their feet extended away from the table," which is why the woman would be at Jesus' feet when standing behind Him.[2]

Although not recorded here in Luke, we know from Matthew's Gospel that Jesus had extended this invitation just prior to the dinner party: "Come to me, all you who are weary and burdened, and I will give you rest. Take my yoke upon you and learn from me, for I am gentle and humble in heart, and you will find rest for your souls. For my yoke is easy and my burden is light" (Matthew 11:28-30).

We don't know for sure, but perhaps the woman in today's reading had heard this invitation. Given her response to Jesus, it seems highly likely.

Rest for Our Souls, Hospitality for a Savior

When the heart is weary, facing the day ahead can be trying and burdensome. Temporary fixes abound, but the antidote is found in deep soul rest as we release our burdens to the only One strong enough to carry them, trusting Him to lighten our load.

Can you recall a time when you craved rest for your soul? Describe it below.

How would you explain what "soul rest" is?

I can think of numerous examples in my life that have triggered a need for deep soul rest. Near the top of that list are moments spent grieving the loss of a loved one. Anxiety over my health is up there as well. But the times that I have craved soul rest the most have been caused by my own sin.

Read Isaiah 59:1-2 and note what it tells us about sin.

Sin stands in the way of intimacy with God. The distance caused by our disobedience creates a strain in our souls. Even though there isn't a day that goes by without a reason to seek forgiveness, I am not always quick to recognize it for what it is. Sometimes a more accurate way of identifying the presence of personal sin is by assessing what is missing.

Galatians 5:22-23 lists nine benefits of communion with God—of union with His Spirit. Read the verses in the margin, and list the benefits or fruit here:

1.

2.

3.

4.

[22]The fruit of the Spirit is love, joy, peace, forbearance, kindness, goodness, faithfulness, [23]gentleness and self-control. Against such things there is no law.
(Galatians 5:22-23)

5.

6.

7.

8.

9.

Is there a particular area that you struggle with? If so, circle it.

I've noticed in my own life that the absence of any of these benefits is always a clue that there might be a need to seek forgiveness. Perhaps the woman who crashed Simon the Pharisee's dinner party recognized this need too.

Although many have tried to label the woman at the dinner party as Mary of Bethany (Luke 10:38-41) or Mary Magdalene (Luke 8:2; 24:10), Warren Wiersbe affirms that she is neither of these women.[4] Although I adore putting the pieces of history together, I rather like that her identity is anonymous. It makes it easier for this sinner to see myself in her actions. Based on Luke's language in Luke 7:37, it is possible that she may have been a prostitute.[5] But whatever her sin was, it was known to the community. Other than that, we know nothing of her except how she responded to Jesus.

Based on her actions, how would you describe this woman?

One commentator observes, "While tears, hair, and kisses showered the Lord's feet, the woman added 'perfume.' The Gospels of Mark and John add that the perfume was pure nard, a highly prized extract from the spikenard plant, native to India and imported at great expense."[6] Song of Solomon references it as a treasured and prized commodity:

> [13]*Your plants are an orchard of pomegranates*
> *with choice fruits,*
> *with henna and nard,*
> [14]*nard and saffron,*
> *calamus and cinnamon,*
> *with every kind of incense tree,*
> *with myrrh and aloes*
> *and all the finest spices.*
>
> (*Song of Solomon* 4:13-14)

In addition, John 12:5 (NKJV) tells us that a flask of oil cost 300 denarii, meaning the woman's perfume would have likely cost her a year's wages. Why do you think the woman was willing to sacrifice so much for the chance to pour her perfume over Jesus' feet?

Read Luke 7:38. Nard wasn't the only thing that anointed Jesus' feet. What else did she use?

What does 1 Corinthians 11:6, 15 tell us about a woman's hair in ancient Israel?

If a woman's hair represented her dignity, what does that say about the woman's actions toward Jesus?

Thinking back to Jesus' invitation of rest for the soul, what could have prompted her to show such humility? (This is an open-ended question to stir our hearts toward Jesus' compassion for us when we are weary.)

Do you find it easy or difficult to respond to Jesus with the same attitude of humility when you have sinned? Explain your response.

Unhindered by social norms and expectations, the woman demonstrated full devotion to the One who was capable of forgiving her sins. Likewise, when we crave rest for our souls, we can find it by bringing our humble hearts to Jesus' feet.

However, she displayed more than just humility and devotion.

In Genesis 18:1-8, Abraham illustrates a beautiful example of hospitality as he welcomes three divine guests. Compare the hospitality of Abraham in that account with the woman and Simon the Pharisee in Luke 7. List each of their actions in the chart on the following page.

Abraham's Actions: Genesis 18:1-8	The Woman's Actions: Luke 7:37-38, 44-46	Simon's Actions: Luke 7:44-46

Abraham meets the expectation for hospitality. Where Simon falls short, the woman exceeds.

What conclusion does Jesus draw in Luke 7:47?

If you identify with this woman, I need you to know that you are in good company. I don't need to pinpoint her identity. Her name is Heather. Her name is yours also. And Jesus is inviting us both to the greatest soul rest known to humanity.

What does Jesus tell her in Luke 7:50? Write His response word for word:

Now, circle the last word above.

Extra Insight

Jesus was careful to point out that it was the woman's faith that saved her, not her works, tears, or love.[7]

Peace. Go in peace. Imagine her face as she left Simon the Pharisee's home. See her body language as she walks back through the streets of Capernaum. Her shoulders a little looser. Her step a little lighter. She sees everything differently now. The moonlight that catches the corner of her own home is brighter. The birdsongs are sweeter. Her breaths are deeper. The burdens she has carried for so long have been lifted. She leaves in peace. And although Luke doesn't reveal the inner workings of her heart after this encounter, I think she also leaves with a determined gleam of devotion in her eyes.

Heart Water

Martin Luther referred to the woman's tears as "heart water."[8] Tears of gratitude, flowing unceasingly from the heart of a woman who craved rest for her soul. Unbreakable affection stems from the recognition of an unrepayable gift. A grateful heart produces true devotion to the One who forgives our sins.

What can you thank Jesus for today? Start with His gift of forgiveness, meditating on His gift of eternal life. Then consider the many blessings He gives us every day. Take some time to thank Him now for all of these things.

If we want to be devoted to Jesus, we'll need to have a heart of gratitude. How can we steep our hearts in thankfulness for what Jesus does for us? Here are a few ideas:

- Say thank-you every day. Include a moment of gratitude in every prayer.
- Start your day by remembering His blessings. Put a note beside your bed to remind you to thank Jesus the first moment you wake up.
- Set a reminder on your phone to pause for a moment of gratitude in the middle of your day.
- Make a gratitude journal to record everything you want to thank Jesus for.
- Meditate on and memorize Scriptures on gratitude.

There is an abundant supply of verses that reference thankfulness; I've listed below a few good places to start. Add any others you may know.

Give thanks to the Lord, for he is good.
His love endures forever.
(Psalm 136:1)

Give thanks in all circumstances; for this is God's will for you in Christ Jesus.
(1 Thessalonians 5:18)

Whatever you do, whether in word or deed, do it all in the name of the Lord Jesus, giving thanks to God the Father through him.
(Colossians 3:17)

[28]Since we are receiving a kingdom that cannot be shaken, let us be thankful, and so worship God acceptably with reverence and awe, [29]for our "God is a consuming fire."
(Hebrews 12:28-29)

Every good and perfect gift is from above, coming down from the Father of the heavenly lights, who does not change like shifting shadows.
(James 1:17)

> A grateful heart produces true devotion to the One who forgives our sins.

Extra Insight

One source reminds us that Jesus' interactions with women were noticeably radical. He crossed cultural barriers to prove that all people were worthy of respect and that He regarded women with care and tenderness. Luke, in particular, records more of Jesus' interactions with women than the other Gospels.[9]

Others:

Let's close today by pouring out our "heart water" to Jesus. Give Him the burdens of your soul, and wait expectantly for Him to fill you with rest.

DAY 3: RESCUE FROM CHAINS (DETERMINED TO LEAVE A LEGACY)

We know him as the author of Luke and Acts in the New Testament, but who exactly was Luke? Let's consider some basic information gleaned from commentator R. T. France that might shed some light on this human writer of God's Word.[1]

Luke, a physician by trade and a self-described historian, uses his skills as a storyteller to our great benefit. Paul names Luke in a list of non-Jewish associates following Colossians 4:11, and we can see clearly from each of the four Gospels that Luke was not one of the chosen Twelve who initially followed Jesus. Luke understood what it meant to be an outsider of a faith community that began within a Jewish nation.

Although Luke is first and foremost a historian, his works read like a narrative with characters, setting, and plot—which is why we have begun each day of this study with The Quick Three. It was Luke's way to focus on these things. He sometimes sacrifices chronology for impact, but he never forfeits truth. France says of Luke that he "is a sophisticated writer who knows how to tell a good story.... But Luke is not just a chronicler of events. He is a man with a message."[2]

Luke had a unique approach to how Jesus' story should be told. Inspired by the breath of God and under Luke's creative genius, it would be a story of God's compassion for the entire world, Jews and Gentiles alike. I like to think it is moments like the one that we will study today that sparked Luke's determination to tell the whole world—in great detail—all that Jesus had done.

Read Luke 8:26-39, and put a placeholder there for future reference.

The Quick Three
What happened?
Where did it happen?
What characters are mentioned in this reading?

Setting the Scene

Commentator R. T. France notes that sailing to the country of Gerasenes would take Jesus and His disciples out of predominantly Jewish areas and into an area on the eastern shore of the Sea of Galilee known as the Decapolis. He further observes that the area was largely occupied by Gentiles and Jesus' disciples would have noticed this fact by the presence of pigs, an animal that was considered unclean for Jews.[3]

Their first step into what might have felt like foreign land brought them face-to-face with a man and his demons. When you imagine this demon-possessed man wandering among the tombs, it might be tempting to picture him in the park-like cemeteries we are accustomed to today, but that would not be altogether accurate. France writes that "ancient tombs were often quite elaborate structures or artificial caves in the hillside, and they would have provided shelter for a man excluded from society."[4]—someone like the demon-possessed man in our story.

Before and After

A goal of this study is for us to embrace the abundant life that Jesus promises in John 10:10: "The thief comes only to steal and kill and destroy. I came that they may have life and have it abundantly" (ESV). Because of that, I want us to think about what we are studying today not in terms of demon-possession but in terms of abundant life—specifically, the difference between the presence and the absence of it.

When you think of the term *abundant life*, what comes to mind?

Describe the man Jesus meets in Luke 8:27-30. Include every detail you find about him.

Extra Insight

Luke 8:30 tells us that the man had a legion of demons. One commentary notes that a Roman legion would include four- to six-thousand troops. Although Luke doesn't clarify how many demons this man was battling, we know it to be a large number.[5] Mark 5:3-5 offers additional insight into the behavior of the demon-possessed man.

Why do you think he had to be bound by chains?

Chains are not always made of iron. They can be unseen, binding us emotionally and mentally. For example, I often struggle with anxiety. You don't face an incurable genetic disorder and the promise of major medical events without anxiety knocking on your door. Statistics say I'm not alone.

It is estimated that almost one-fifth of the American population struggles with anxiety issues.[6] Anxiety is an overall feeling of nervousness, dread, or unease that can manifest itself in a variety of ways, including, but certainly not limited to, irritability, muscle tension, chronic pain, difficulty concentrating, insomnia, headaches, heart palpitations, and difficulty breathing.

Anxiety can be the difference between saying yes to a Friday night social gathering or staying in to try and manage your oncoming panic attack. It can be the thing can keeps you up at night, the thing that keeps you down in the morning, and the thing that keeps you from chasing your dreams. Regardless of how it manifests, anxiety keeps you in chains by keeping you from abundant living.

Anxiety isn't the only thing that keeps us from living a full life.

What else might get in the way of Jesus' promise of living fully?

Would you define your way of life today as *abundant*? Why or why not?

Look up and read each Scripture carefully, writing a brief characteristic of abundant living based on the truth(s) you find there. I have done the first one for you as an example.

Psalm 1:1-3   **endurance and fulfillment of my soul**

Isaiah 58:11

Galatians 5:1

1 Timothy 6:18-19

Now, combine the characteristics you listed to write a biblical definition of abundant living:

Abundant living in Jesus is . . .

Where the
enemy takes
us to break us,
Jesus takes us
to heal us.

Luke 8:29 tells us that the demon drove the man into "solitary places." Flip back to Luke 4:42 and you'll recognize that we've seen that phrase before (some versions use the word *secluded* or *deserted*). It's where Jesus sought rest and renewal with His heavenly Father. Where the enemy takes us to break us, Jesus takes us to heal us.

What does Psalm 107:14 tell us about what God does?

Read Luke 8:32-33. What happened to the demons that had tormented the man?

Now, describe the man as we find him in Luke 8:35-36. List every detail given about him after Jesus has cleansed him of the demons.

Jesus is the Divine Chain-Breaker. There is no darkness He can't free us from, no hold He can't shatter. The thief will come to steal and destroy, we can be sure of that. But we must remember that the enemy is doomed to destruction and submits to Christ. When we trust Jesus with our lives, He will redeem every attempt to break us; and we will be left to sit at His feet and marvel in his powerful grace and mercy.

We have seen other encounters where Jesus has requested the silence of those benefiting from His power, but in this instance He does something different.

In Luke 8:38-39, what does Jesus command that the freed man do? Why do you think Jesus' preference is different here?

How does the man's response compare with the words of Psalm 107:2-3 (in the margin)?

²Let the redeemed of the Lord tell their story—
those he redeemed from the hand of the foe,
³those he gathered from the lands, from east and west, from north and south.
(Psalm 107:2-3)

Leaving a Legacy of Faith

Yesterday my neighbor stopped by with a surprise gift. You should know that she is my Bible study leader. Every week we gather with a small group of ladies to read, study, and discuss the truth of God's Word. Her gifts are always thoughtful, and they usually point me to our shared faith in Christ. This gift was no different.

It was a simple gold-banded ring. On it was the inscription *worth it.*

The ring wasn't fancy, but the message was profound. We are worthy of making a difference in the world simply because we serve a King who is worthy of all praise. I'm wearing the ring now as I am thinking of you. Jesus makes your story worthy.

The story of the demon-possessed man from the Gerasenes was worth it, and your story is worth it as well. Regardless of your past, God can use you. God can use *anyone* to leave a legacy for His kingdom.

If you have a pulse, you have a purpose. The two-step process to fulfilling it is quite simple, actually.

Step 1: Follow Jesus

If you don't already know Jesus as your personal Savior, I invite you to trust Him now. He can break every chain that is keeping you from abundant living. You can pray this simple prayer now and know that it will be received in the heavenlies with rejoicing. Or you can adapt it as a reaffirmation of your commitment to follow Him.

Jesus, I know that I am a sinner in need of Your salvation. I know that You are the Son of God, who came down to earth to live as a human. I know you willingly sacrificed Yourself on the cross so that I might have abundant life now and forever. I know that You rose from the dead and ascended into heaven. And I know that You will return one day to reign over all of earth and heaven in God's holy kingdom. Until that day, fasten my heart to yours. Teach me to walk in union with You and Your will so that I may know You and love You more and more and leave a lasting legacy for Your kingdom. I pray these things in Your holy and precious name. Amen.

Step 2: Leave a Legacy

Our response to being rescued by Jesus should make us determined to leave a legacy of His good news. Jesus' promise is the same today as it was over two thousand years ago: He'll be the chain-breaker. We'll be a legacy-maker. Following the Divine Chain-Breaker empowers us to be lasting legacy-makers.

Jesus makes you worthy of influence. So my last question for you today is this: *what kind of legacy are you leaving?*

Following the Divine Chain-Breaker empowers us to be lasting legacy-makers.

Here are a few questions you can take to Jesus in prayer:

- Who in your church, workplace, or neighborhood needs a little encouragement to be courageous?
- Who needs the gift of biblical wisdom and solid teaching from God's Word?
- What areas in your community are in need of acts of service?
- Who needs to know the love of Christ?

May we step forward as Jesus-driven, legacy-making women!

DAY 4: RESCUE FROM UNBELIEF (DETERMINED TO POSSESS UNWAVERING FAITH)

I was twelve years old when I accepted Jesus as my Savior. I did not grow up in a church home, but my mother took my brother and me to Easter service every year, so I was at least somewhat familiar with the scene. I was eleven when she died. Back then, her death was a medical mystery, but we now know that I inherited the genetic disorder, Vascular Ehlers-Danlos Syndrome, from her. This is what took her life at the age of thirty-seven.

The summer after her funeral, my good friend Sarah invited me to church camp with her youth group. I said yes. I had no idea what I was getting into, but it sounded like fun; and I was in sore need of a reason to smile. I told no one of my feelings, but I remember climbing the church bus with heavy steps that matched the weight of my heart.

Jesus was waiting for me in the Bible classes, worship sessions, and prayer groups that week. When I think back to the final invitation night, I can't tell you what the pastor said, but I remember every song that we sang. It didn't all make perfect sense, but it didn't need to. Faith overrules logic. I only knew there was a gaping hole where my heart once was that only Jesus could fill. I was ready to give it to Him. I was too nervous to walk down to the altar where counselors were waiting with kind eyes and warm hugs; my friend Eric noticed, so he stood up and walked with me. I barely knew him, but even youth recognize when Jesus is stirring.

Daughter, your faith has saved you.

I felt those words echo deep into my shattered heart, and it settled something there that had been restless long before my mother had died. When we returned, I bounced my way off the bus and headed home with joy I couldn't describe. Not long after, my youth leader asked me when I would be ready to give my public confession of faith. I'm sure I looked at her with wide and confused eyes, because she replied to my unspoken question with, "Heather, all you have to do is tell everyone why you believe in Jesus."

My answer was simple: He had saved me.

Read Luke 8:40-56, and put a placeholder there for future reference.

The Quick Three
What happened?
Where did it happen?
What characters are mentioned in this reading?

Setting the Scene

Although Luke doesn't explicitly tell us, scholars agree that at this point Jesus had returned to Capernaum, his ministry headquarters for now.[1] Luke bounces between the two climactic accounts of Jairus's daughter and the bleeding woman, but that's intentional. Remember that Luke is a storyteller, not just a fact-deliverer. And we'll see in a moment that he has a point to make with this strategic unfolding.

Jairus's duties at the synagogue included presiding over the elders and appointing people to pray, read the Scriptures, and teach.[2] One source notes that the mentioning of his name "indicates that he was a leading figure in the community," not just a synagogue ruler.[3] However, prominence doesn't provide immunity from hardship; so everything stopped for this well-respected man as his only daughter, one who had brought him twelve years of joy, faced a deathly illness.

The bleeding woman likely suffered from a menstrual disorder, for Luke tells us that she "had been subject to bleeding for twelve years, but no one could heal her" (8:43). As one source explains, "A continual flow of blood from her womb rendered her perpetually unclean (Lev. 15:25-30)."[4] She understood well the feeling of being shunned.

Twelve years of joy and twelve years of sorrow. The contrast between these two scenarios is striking, but the need is the same. Jesus, the Great Physician, is capable of healing all ailments: physical, mental, and spiritual. The only thing we bring to the table is our belief.

Only Believe

In a world dominated by our senses, we are accustomed to putting our faith in the tangible. It's easy to place our trust in things that we can physically touch. Believing in something that we can't see with our own eyes is another matter altogether.

In three sentences or less, describe why you believe in Jesus. If you're not sure if you believe in Jesus, that's okay. Describe what it would take for you to believe in Him.

Because Jairus was a synagogue leader, we can assume that he was godly, but let's consider what else we might infer about this well-respected man who was willing to fall at Jesus' feet.

Given both Jairus's prominent position in the community and his actions toward Jesus in verses 41 and 42, describe what kind of man you think he might be:

We can take comfort in the fact that Jesus does not tarry. When there is a need, He determines to meet it. But His time line doesn't always fit our expectations, as we see in the following verses.

As faithful as he was, how might Jairus have felt as he watched Jesus' encounter and exchange with the bleeding woman (vv. 43-48)?

Visually construct the scene set before us in your mind: Jesus is on his way to Jairus's home. His popularity has grown, so the masses follow where He walks. He is surrounded by a crowd of onlookers; some are already devotees, and others are simply curious. Through the chaos of hustling feet and clamoring voices, a desperate woman fights her way to the fringe of His garment.

The Lord gave the Old Testament Israelites specific instructions about their garment details. Read Numbers 15:37-41 to discover the requirement for tassels. Why did God insist upon this?

Extra Insight

One source notes that because the woman was considered unclean due to her bleeding disorder, she "could not touch or be touched, was probably now divorced or had never married, and was marginal to the rest of Jewish society."[5]

One commentary reminds us of an important detail to note here: "In those days, devout Jews wore an outer tunic that had four tassels hanging from the hem. Traditionally, the tassels represented the Lord's commands (Num. 15:37-40; Deut. 22:12). The woman probably touched the tassel hanging over Jesus' shoulder."[6] As the passage from Numbers informs us, the wearing of tassels was meant to help God's people remember His commands.

How would you characterize or describe the woman's demeanor as she falls before Jesus' feet in Luke 8:47?

Do you think she was trembling because she was embarrassed? Is there another reason why she might be trembling?

We've noted already that due to her bleeding disorder, this woman had been considered unclean for twelve years. Because she would not have been allowed to participate in the traditional Jewish worship setting, she was also prohibited from publicly sharing her faith for that entire time. There was surely trepidation in her voice from fear, but perhaps she was trembling from anticipation or excitement as well. The Savior had indeed saved her. No longer was she forced to live as an outcast. For a woman who had not received physical touch in twelve years, one touch of the Savior's hem had healed every measure of sorrow and misery. Oh, what a testimony to give!

Extra Insight

By touching a bleeding woman and a dead body, Jesus risks ritual defilement, a significant taboo in the Jewish faith.[7] Numbers 19:11-16 and Leviticus 15:25-30 explain what was ultimately at stake: separation from the nation of Israel. Jesus' choice to touch them anyway foreshadows His willingness and authority to take on the sin of the world.

Luke 8:47 reveals that the woman, unnoticed by the Savior, told the crowd why she touched Jesus and how she had been healed. What is Jesus' response in verse 48?

In your own words, describe either how Jesus has healed you of something, whether physical or emotional, or how it feels knowing that you cannot go unnoticed by Jesus.

In the next verse Luke turns our attention back to Jairus's daughter, and we see that the situation has intensified. If he was at all impatient before when Jesus stopped to help the bleeding woman, he might have been downright livid at this new update. But we can know with certainty that Jesus had not forgotten his daughter.

Note the verb tense change in reference to the girl's health status from Luke 8:42 to Luke 8:49. What does this imply?

If the change in tense from "was dying" to "is dead" isn't enough to solidify the desperation of this situation, there is another clue that tells us that the girl has, in fact, died.

Compare Luke 8:55 with James 2:26. What evidence is found that would declare her dead?

What does the crowd encourage Jairus to do in Luke 8:49?

When faced with a situation that feels hopeless, it can be tempting to give up. Death doesn't come only with the cessation of breath. I wonder, are you facing the death of a relationship today? The death of a marriage? A job? A dream? Or is there something in your life about which you have decided to simply not bother Jesus with anymore? His timing might not make sense to you right now, but Jesus has not forgotten your plea for help.

Rewrite Jesus' reply in Luke 8:50 word for word:

Do you think there is a difference between *believing in God* and *believing God*? Why or why not?

Believing in God vs. Believing God

God wants us to believe *in* Him, but He also wants us to *believe* Him. There is a difference. The characters from today's reading help us find it.

Each character in today's reading responds to Jesus in three different ways. Compare each of their responses by completing the chart on the following page.

Character	How they respond to Jesus
The bleeding woman *Luke 8:43-44, 47-48*	
Jairus *Luke 8:41-42, 50*	
The crowd *Luke 8:49, 52, 53*	

The woman of bold faith. The synagogue ruler who was faithful but afraid. And the crowd who shook their heads and said "don't bother." Which one of these three do you identify with most *today*?

What does Jesus tell Jairus's daughter in Luke 8:54?

For those who seek Jesus, there is an original moment when He calls us to arise. Mine came when I was twelve years old. It was time then for me to stand and proclaim my faith in His name. But it didn't end there. Over and over again, Jesus has asked me to arise. *Arise and worship* My name. *Arise and love My people. Arise and step into the unknown. Arise and know that I am good. Arise and believe that what I tell you is true. Arise and trust Me to find you in the darkness. Arise and follow Me into the light.*

Abundant life is found in our choice to arise because every time we choose to believe Jesus, we fall in love with Him a little more. An unspoken trust transaction happens when we take Jesus at His word. Authentic belief breeds refined intimacy. One daughter discovered this when Jesus brought her back to life. Another one confirmed it when she leaped for His tassel.

Read Hebrews 11:6 in the margin. According to this verse, what are the results or outcomes of our faith?

Without faith it is impossible to please God, because anyone who comes to him must believe that he exists and that he rewards those who earnestly seek him.

(Hebrews 11:6)

How would you define your relationship with Jesus today?
Circle your answer.

I've just met Him.

I'm getting to know Him better.

I know Him intimately and want to continue growing in intimacy.

Finding a Bold and Unwavering Faith

I have reacted like all three characters at various times in my faith journey. I've chosen not to bother Jesus with something I was sure He had forgotten. I've tried to be faithful, but on the inside I was shaking with fear. And I've taken hopeful leaps that were propelled only by unwavering faith. It's this last one that I want more of. What about you?

R. T. France notes another detail that encourages me to be bold in my faith. With the exception of the reference to a woman as a daughter of Abraham in Luke 13:16, Jesus' interaction with the bleeding woman is the only time in Luke that Jesus addresses a woman as *daughter*. This wasn't an accident. It was meant to imply intimacy and closeness.[8] Whatever she knew of Jesus before she found Him among the crowd, it is clear from her actions and Jesus' response that her faith was not shallow. Shallow faith doesn't prompt one to walk headfirst into a crowd that has already rejected her. But a determined, authentic belief does.

Many in the crowd likely believed *in* Jesus. They had seen Him perform miracles already. Maybe they had heard Him preach on the shores of Galilee. They had heard stories of His extraordinary baptism in the Jordan River. But did they *believe* Him? Did they believe that what He said was true?

There is a difference between *believing in God* and *believing God*. What lies between is where deep and boundless faith is built, and the reward on the other side is intimacy with the One who can heal all that is broken. When we determine to believe Jesus, rather than just believe in Him, we'll develop a close and personal relationship with Him. Unwavering faith is built by *believing* Jesus.

> When we determine to believe Jesus, rather than just believe in Him, we'll develop a close and personal relationship with Him.

Listed below and on the following page are just a handful of the promises Jesus makes to us. Look up each Scripture and fill in the blank(s). If there is a promise that you have a hard time believing, settle on it for a moment.

Jesus promises_____. (Matthew 11:28-30)

Jesus promises _____ life. (John 10:10)

Jesus promises _____ life. (John 3:16)

Jesus promises the _____ _____ to help us share His love with the world. (Acts 1:8)

Jesus promises that He will _____ for us. (John 14:2-3)

Close today by asking Jesus to help you believe Him:

Jesus, I want to possess unwavering faith because I know the reward is a close and personal relationship with You. I confess to You the promises I struggle to believe (name them). Help me to trust You completely. Amen.

DAY 5: RESCUE FROM APATHY (DETERMINED TO SOLVE PROBLEMS)

> "Let God's promises shine on your problems."
> —Corrie ten Boom[1]

After closing yesterday's lesson by meditating on the promises of Jesus, it feels appropriate to open today with this wise quotation from Corrie ten Boom. This news will undoubtedly not come as a shock, but you and I will face many obstacles in our quest to live like Jesus. Life is hard. The enemy is relentless. And we humans are easily fatigued.

Jesus has already taught us the importance of seeking rest and renewal, and a healthy balance of hard work with intentional repose should be something we all strive for. But what about the moments when walking away from our responsibilities to seek respite isn't possible? I'm picturing in my mind the mother of a newborn who hasn't had three consecutive hours of sleep in two months. Or the conscientious executive who works sixteen-hour days because over one hundred employees rely on her dedication to feed their families.

I'm quite convinced that we won't polish the perfect balance between our responsibilities and rest until we are living in total communion with God in heaven. Until then, there will be some days that allow for restoration and others that will flat-out call for miracles.

Jesus' disciples are about to learn that they can still fulfill their roles even when their resources are limited. When we determine to rely on Jesus' strength and not our own, anything is possible.

Read Luke 9:10-17, and put a placeholder there for future reference.

<table>
<tr><td colspan="2" align="center">**The Quick Three**</td></tr>
<tr><td>What happened?</td></tr>
<tr><td>Where did it happen?</td></tr>
<tr><td>What characters are mentioned in this reading?</td></tr>
</table>

Setting the Scene

The beginning verses of Luke 9 reveal that Jesus' twelve disciples had been sent out with a definitive list of tasks resembling Jesus' manifesto that we studied together in Luke 4. Disciples of Jesus have jobs to do to reflect His love for the world. But given that verse 10 tells us they "withdrew by themselves," it might be reasonable to assume that they returned from their initial mission worn out and weary, with no end in sight for the assignment at hand. Mark 6:30-31 reveals another angle of this story and Jesus' tender heart toward making sure they found time to rest:

> 30The apostles gathered around Jesus and reported to him all they had done and taught. 31Then, because so many people were coming and going that they did not even have a chance to eat, he said to them, "Come with me by yourselves to a quiet place and get some rest."
>
> (Mark 6:30-31)

There would be no rest for the weary. The crowds were hungry, physically and spiritually. But Jesus, having compassion on both His disciples and the crowds that pursued them, had a plan.

One commentator remarks that the traditional location for this scene is Tabgha, a Galilean coastal town just southwest of Capernaum, but that scholars are more recently endorsing the remote plains just north of Bethsaida as the setting for today's miracle.[2] It matters not to our goal for today whether they were in Tabgha or north of Bethsaida, as long as we remember what Luke 9:12 confirms, that the area they were in was isolated and far-removed from provisions and supplies.

It was the perfect location for Jesus to flex His miracle muscles, and it's the perfect place for us to meet Him when we are running on empty.

Working with Open Hands

Today's reading reveals both a human and a divine response to weariness and need.

Consider how Jesus' disciples might have felt after returning from a season of preaching and healing (Luke 9:6, 10). Can you recall a time when you felt a similar way?

When you are tired and weary, how concerned do you tend to be for the needs of others?

How do the disciples respond to the influx of crowds in Luke 9:12?

Which factors do you think are at play with the disciples' request to send the crowd away?

____ They were tired of engaging with people and wanted some down time.

____ They were aware that it would be near impossible to find enough food for the crowd in the remote area where they were.

____ Both of the previous answers.

Write Jesus' response in Luke 9:13 word for word below:

One of the things I appreciate most about Jesus' disciples is that they help me to recognize myself in their behaviors. At first, we expect them to be rather unique and especially gifted because Jesus chose *them* above all others. And then we realize that they are no different than you and me. They are made with flesh and bones just as we are, and they carry the same desires and weaknesses that we do. The lessons we see them learning apply to our lives as well. We can let Jesus teach us as we watch Him teach them.

So, let's soak up knowledge from their experience by reversing this picture. If the disciples' choices are an example of what not to do, let's consider a response that would honor God the most.

"Nothing will be impossible with God."

(Luke 1:37 ESV)

Keeping Luke 1:37 in mind (see the margin), fill in the chart on the following page with responses that you think would have pleased Jesus in each scenario.

Situation	Disciples' Response	A Jesus-centered approach
The disciples are tired and weary, but ministry doesn't stop; and a crowd in need of healing invades their resting place.	"Send the crowds away, Jesus!"	
Resources to help the crowd are virtually nonexistent where the disciples are.	"The surrounding villages can help them better than we can."	
Jesus asks them to do the impossible by feeding the crowd.	"That's impossible! We don't have the provisions for that!"	

As my son was learning upper elementary math, I would sometimes tell him that Jesus is the perfect math teacher because He's exceedingly good at multiplication. If we are working with only seven small resources, Jesus can multiply it into five thousand. The lesson we are learning from the disciples today is to hold our meager resources with open hands, lift them toward heaven, and wait for Jesus to work a miracle.

Is there an area in your family, work, or ministry life that has limited resources? If so, take a moment now to pray over it, offering your resources with open hands to Jesus. Write your prayer in the margin, if you like.

This scene was not just an opportunity for Jesus to teach of His abundant provision. There was something else He needed His disciples to learn.

Choose three of the verses below to read, and note what each teaches about caring for others:

Proverbs 22:9

Luke 6:38

Philippians 2:3-4

Hebrews 13:16

1 John 3:17

Glance again at Jesus' command in Luke 9:13. When the disciples told Jesus the task before them was impossible, He asked *them* to make it possible. Has Jesus ever asked *you* to do the impossible? If so, describe it briefly below:

Offering another perspective on this encounter, John 6:6 reminds us that when He tested His disciples, Jesus also knew exactly what He was going to do: "He asked this only to test him, for he already had in mind what he was going to do." When He calls us to do the impossible, He always has a plan. Pay attention to the details swirling around you when you are in the middle of a situation that feels hopeless. God may be calling you to solve a problem, but He will also provide miraculous resources.

Compare Luke 9:10-17, our passage for today, to 2 Kings 4:42-44, and jot down any similarities you find:

Extra Insight

Jesus assumes a common posture as He prays over the food for the crowd. We see this posture also in 1 Kings 8:54: "When Solomon had finished all these prayers and supplications to the Lord, he rose from before the altar of the Lord, where he had been kneeling with his hands spread out toward heaven."

This snippet from the Old Testament would have been familiar to Jewish observers in the crowd eating loaves and fishes. This wasn't the first time God had performed a miracle of abundant provision, and it wouldn't be the last.

See It, Fill It

When the disciples started this journey of carrying out Jesus' mission, they had nothing. We read that Jesus told them: "Take nothing for the journey—no staff, no bag, no bread, no money, no extra shirt" (Luke 9:3). So they had nothing to offer the hungry crowd. Yet at the end of this long day of caring for the needs of others, each disciple held a basket overflowing with leftover food. They had to learn that acknowledging their weaknesses released a flood of Jesus' power and provision.

Whatever you have on your plate this week, know that Jesus always works from a place of abundance. He is never not enough. He will always have more than enough of what you need. Joy, peace, patience, love, compassion, energy, wisdom, or tangible provision—He has more than enough of it for you. The only things we can give back to Him in abundance are our time, our worship, our thanksgiving, and our obedience.

Today's obedience looks like taking care of others' needs. Jesus was clear about His expectation for the disciples: *you feed them*. When we have direct access to the power of the Creator of the universe, we can't afford the luxury of bypassing the needs of others. We must fix things, solve problems, and care for those in our path. As followers of Jesus, we are called to recognize and resource the unmet needs of others.

As followers of Jesus, we are called to recognize and resource the unmet needs of others.

Jesus was a problem-solver, and He asks us to be the same. What are some of the ways we can meet the needs of others in our homes, churches, workplaces, nation, and world?

I'd love to hear your ideas. Here are a few of my own. We can meet the needs of others by:

- Contributing financially (Ask Jesus where your money can best help others.)
- Serving tangibly (Look for areas that need hands-on acts of service.)
- Motivating collectively (Invite others to solve problems with you.)

I invite you to close today by prayerfully considering how you might take steps to meet needs in one of these three ways. First, check one or more areas where you see a need, and briefly describe the specific need in the column on the left. Then in the column on the right, write the appropriate letter to indicate whether you will fill it by (a) contributing financially, (b) serving tangibly, or (c) motivating collectively. Make notes about your next steps, if you like.

I see a need in my . . .   The need: I will fill it by . . .

__home

__church

__workplace

__nation

__world

Let's trust Jesus to miraculously provide resources as we identify and meet the needs of those around us.

VIDEO VIEWER GUIDE: WEEK 3

Luke 8:22-25

When the storm of life hit, we may feel like Jesus is _____.

Even when our lives are notoriously unpredictable, Jesus remains predictable, constant, and _____ _____.

Hebrews 13:8

Jesus is more concerned with our _____ than our _____.

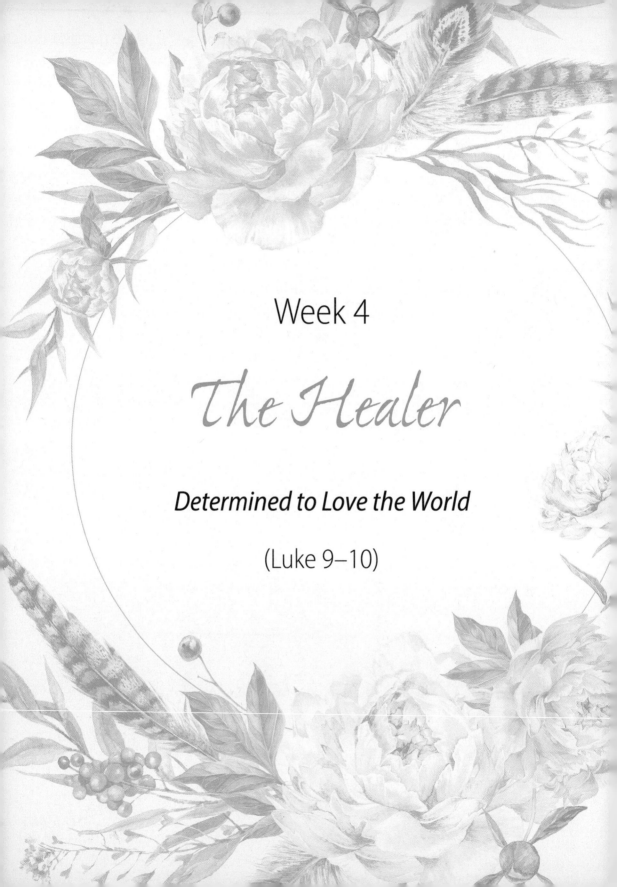

Week 4

The Healer

Determined to Love the World

(Luke 9–10)

> Since we are surrounded by such a great cloud of witnesses, let us throw off everything that hinders and the sin that so easily entangles. And let us run with perseverance the race marked out for us.
>
> (Hebrews 12:1)

I have a magnet hanging on my refrigerator with a popularized version of a quotation from Winston Churchill. It says, "Never, never, never give up." I bought it when I was sleep-deprived and covered in spit up. I needed all the pep talks I could get in those days, although it wasn't just because I had a newborn. I had a newborn whom I couldn't feed well. No one told me that nursing would be difficult. I am not exaggerating when I tell you it was one of the hardest things I've ever had to do.

There will be moments in our lives when we will have to clinch our jaw and determine to keep moving forward anyway. Our circumstances will be challenging, our bodies will be weary, and our hearts will be full of doubt. In those moments it will be unquestioningly easier to walk away.

You've probably experienced similar moments just in the past three weeks of our study together. Stay the course. Dig your heels in. Don't give up. Why? Not because I am encouraging you to, but because this is the choice Jesus made. He determined to move forward anyway. His convictions were so strong that He never, never, never walked away from being obedient to God's will. And at the heart of His convictions were you and me, and understanding of those moments when the world would prefer that we give up. Let's show the world Jesus' way instead and live determined.

As I noted, my magnet with the popularized saying is not altogether accurate. What Winston Churchill actually said was, "Never give in, never give in, never, never, never, never—in nothing, great or small, large or petty—never give in except to convictions of honour and good sense."[1]

He wasn't speaking of a spiritual battle, but of Great Britain's progress during World War II. In the same speech he also said, "Do not let us speak of darker days: let us speak rather of sterner days. These are not dark days; these are great days—the greatest days our country has ever lived; and we must all thank God that we have been allowed, each of us according to our stations, to play a part in making these days memorable in the history of our race."[2]

I think Jesus would agree. The writer of Hebrews goes on to call us to follow His example:

> [1b]And let us run with perseverance the race marked out for us, [2]fixing our eyes on Jesus, the pioneer and perfecter of faith. For the joy set before him he endured the cross, scorning its shame, and sat down at the right hand of the throne of God.
>
> (Hebrews 12:1b-2)

DAY 1: HEALING OUR PAST

I grew up in the public library. My aunt raised me after my mother died, and her single-mom lifestyle meant that I spent many afternoons getting cozy with the Dewey decimal system. I didn't mind in the least. I'd read through one entire section of the library and move right on to the other, barely noticing when it was time to meet her outside when she got off work. My modest, hometown library was a safe place to hide as I grieved for my mom, but it also gave me a deep appreciation for a well-written story.

In every good story there is a climax. If the author is clever enough, it will be an unexpected one. It's the moment that makes you gasp when a crucial plot element is revealed, and everything changes for the characters and for you from that point forward. It takes a consistent build-up of intensity to reach that point, and we're starting a similar ascent this week in our study of Luke.

You and I know the climax of this story, but that doesn't make it any less clever or dramatic. When the story is God's Word, it speaks directly into our lives no matter how many times we've read it. Luke, ever the storyteller, is about to pull back the curtain on a moment when Peter realizes something you and I already know. Let's allow his revelation to be as fresh for us today as it was for him two thousand years ago.

Read Luke 9:18-20, and put a placeholder there for future reference.

The Quick Three
What happened?
Where did it happen?
What characters are mentioned in this reading?

Setting the Scene

If I asked to borrow a bit of olive oil from your pantry, I'm guessing you would probably have some on hand. What we know as a simple, everyday ingredient was used in ancient Israel to designate a significant honor. One commentary explains, "In many ancient Near Eastern cultures, a person receiving special recognition would participate in a ceremony in which a small amount of olive oil was poured over the head. The honor came as a reward for valor on the battlefield or victory over a national enemy. The Hebrews eventually reserved it for commissioning their national leader. In Israel, 'the Lord's anointed' (e.g., 1 Sam. 2:10) was none other than the reigning king."[1]

If you're thinking that this honor should also apply to Jesus, you would be right. He is worthy of all honor and glory, and we're about to learn why. We are only diving into three short verses today, but that's intentional. In them is a rather hefty question, and we want to treat it carefully.

At the end of Week 2, we left Jesus feeding the five thousand, which would be His last major act of ministry in Galilee.[2] He now has His mind set on something else, which we will discover together later this week. But in this moment, He wants to know the gossip—about Him, that is.

In Luke 9:18 Jesus is essentially saying: "People are talking. What does the world say about me?" Let's begin today by exploring this question ourselves.

The Anointed One

Just as in His own day, the world has plenty to say about Jesus today. From our neighbors and coworkers to the nightly news and social media, we find all kinds of opinions about Jesus.

> What does our world say about Jesus? How does our society view Jesus today? (Draw upon what you've heard and read, or go ahead and Google it if you want.)

Now, let's back up some two thousand years and discover what first-century Palestine said about Jesus. Gossip about Jesus swirled around three possible identities for who he was.

> Read Luke 9:19 and list the three identities below:

1.

2.

3.

Glance back at Luke 9:7-9 to see evidence of the gossip from Herod's perspective. As we remember from Week 1 of our study, John the Baptist was an enemy of Herod Antipas because he spoke publicly against Herod's actions; and Herod promptly imprisoned John (Luke 3:19-20). He also had John killed (Mark 6:17-29). Now he fears that Jesus is John, raised from the dead and coming back to taunt him once more (see also Mark 6:16).

The Jews in Jesus' day would remember well the promise from the prophet Malachi.

Read Malachi 4:5-6 in the margin, and note below the prophecy mentioned in verse 5.

Jesus wasn't John the Baptist, and He wasn't Elijah returned. Could He simply be a new prophet?

The Jews of that time were hungry for prophetic voices, since they had not heard any in four hundred years.[3] They knew that God had spoken to His people through the prophets, so many naturally believed that Jesus was a prophet.

Look up Luke 4:24 and reread Jesus' words to his hometown synagogue in Nazareth. How does He refer to Himself there?

We've already discussed that a prophet was simply one who "had a special gift of declaring and interpreting God's message."[4] Although Jesus certainly fits this mold, and even refers to Himself as such, He is infinitely more than that.

Read the verses below and note what each tells us about Jesus:

Luke 2:11

Luke 2:26

Luke 4:41

Who does Peter say Jesus is in Luke 9:20?

Depending on which translation you are reading from, Peter answers that Jesus is "God's Messiah," "The Christ [or Messiah] of God."

What does God's Messiah mean? R. T. France offers this explanation:

"Messiah" means "anointed." In the Old Testament kings and priests were anointed for their special offices. "The Lord's anointed" became a familiar term for the Davidic king. After the fall of the monarchy there was a growing hope of a new king of the line of David, and while the term "messiah" was not used in this way within the Old Testament, it became more common in later Jewish literature. Different groups had different notions of what sort of deliverer God would send to his people, but the kingly ideal was fundamental for most and led many to see the Messiah's mission in essentially political terms, especially in the light of Israel's subjection to Rome.[5]

There were many anointed ones throughout the history of Israel, and many of the people expected Jesus to be a delivering king. But Jesus would supersede all of the previous anointed ones as *the* Anointed One, the Savior of humankind. We will see His anointing as king when He returns to reign over all of earth and heaven! Praise be to Jesus Christ, the Messiah, Savior, and Anointed One!

When Jesus asked Peter who He was, He was drawing a line between opinion and conviction.[6] He asks the same of us today.

Who do *you* say that Jesus is? Write below who you believe Him to be, who He is to you personally, and what that means for your life.

Jesus, you are . . .

In what ways does what you wrote contradict with what the world says about Jesus?

Here in Luke 9, Jesus isn't just separating opinion from conviction by asking for a declaration. He's creating a divide between the past and the future—for Peter and for us. Once we declare who Jesus is, everything changes. As the Apostle Paul wrote, "If anyone is in Christ, the new creation has come: The old has gone, the new is here!" (2 Corinthians 5:17).

The Most Determined Choice You Will Ever Make

Fourteen hundred years before Jesus would set foot on earth, God's people were asked to step their feet into a flooding river.[7] One side of the river held their past. The other side held their future. Stepping into the flood held the declaration of their faith. The third chapter of the Book of Joshua tells of the Israelite journey into the Promised Land. If they had stayed east of the Jordan River and held on to their past, they never would have made it to the land of milk and honey.

The characters change, but the story remains virtually the same. When we declare our faith in Jesus, He will lead us to abundant life. But to embrace our future with Christ, we must be willing to let Him heal our past.

Sin. Grief. Loss. Mistakes. Betrayal. Hurt. Disappointment. Fear. Anxiety. *Brokenness.* My past holds all of these, and yours probably does too. Within

Extra Insight

Examples of anointings can be found in Exodus 30:30; 1 Samuel 15:1; 2 Samuel 2:4; and also in Luke 4:18 where Jesus proclaims that God has anointed Him. Acts 10:37-38 also speaks of how God anointed Jesus.

To embrace our future with Christ, we must be willing to let Him heal our past.

each of us there is an immense need for rescue that can be met only by God's Anointed One.

With these very thoughts on my mind before dawn one morning, I padded into the kitchen with slow steps and socked feet. The blessed aroma from the coffee machine rose to greet me, and my eyes saw my surroundings with a bit more clarity as I stepped onto the back porch. I watched the sky shift and move and glow, coming alive with every stroke of God's hand. I heard the birds chirp their morning greeting and felt the fresh dew tickle my feet as I walked to clip a few flowers from my garden.

The scene around me echoed truth from the pages of Scripture: everything of that morning was new. A new sunrise, a new birdsong. New drops of water on the grass and new blooms in my garden. In all of these things was a reminder of God's promise to make all things new, even the things from my past that keep me from moving forward.

His creation echoes a whisper from Jesus that beckons to us: you can start over, you can try again, you are not defined by your past. What happened yesterday does not have to carry forward to today.

New beginnings. Is this not the glorious walk of the Christian life? Jesus is in the business of daily do-overs, and He's rather fond of second chances that are rooted in His grace.

All it takes is the difference between an opinion and a conviction, a declaration that Jesus Christ is the Messiah of the world, the Messiah of your life. To acknowledge that Jesus is the Anointed One is to affirm that He can and will heal your past and give you hope for the future. This may very well be the most determined choice you will ever make: to reject what the world says about Jesus and proclaim His truth for yourself. And it brings an abundant life that this world will never be able to imitate.

What from your past needs healing from Jesus today?

Close today by meditating on these words from one of my favorite worship songs, "Holy and Anointed One" by John Barrett. Begin by saying the name of Jesus, and then let the words wash over your past as they bring healing and hope. (If you want, find the song online and meditate on the full lyrics as you listen.)

Your name is like honey on my lips,
Your Spirit like water to my soul.[8]

Jesus, we praise you, God's Holy and Anointed One!

DAY 2: EMBRACING OUR PRESENT

"Life is a given until it isn't."
—Amanda Bible Williams, *She Reads Truth*[1]

"But that's just ten years from now," I whispered. My husband squeezed my hand as we listened to my geneticist. Instantly, my mind flashed to what I thought I should be doing in ten years. Attending my son's high school graduation. Celebrating my twenty-third wedding anniversary. Figuring out how to empty nest without a copious amount of tissues. All of these givens were now...not.

"I know it's hard to accept, but the life expectancy of someone with Vascular Ehlers-Danlos is usually cut short," said the doctor with the soft voice from across the table. "Major medical events are guaranteed."

I squeezed Tom's hand in return and swiftly nodded. The anxious thoughts didn't hit me just then. They waited until the house was quiet and the sky was black to invade whatever shreds of peace still remained. This was difficult news to hear.

I've often said that anxiety is simply the fear of the unknown. The problem is that we think we *know* what should lie in the *unknown*. Human expectations for earthly life abound. Education, marriage, family, occupation, goals, lifestyle. None of these are bad things, until they come between you and your relationship with the One who gave them to you. If we are wise, we'll learn to release our expectations of them now in exchange for the real prize.

Will it be easy? No. Worth it? Absolutely. Jesus is about to show us why.

Read Luke 9:21-27, and put a placeholder there for future reference.

The Quick Three
What happened?
Where did it happen?
What characters are mentioned in this reading?

Setting the Scene

We're picking up right where we left off yesterday, so there isn't too much of a scene to set for today. Peter has just declared Jesus as the Messiah, but there is still wisdom to be imparted from the Teacher. Luke doesn't specify the location of their talk, but Matthew and Mark pinpoint it in Caesarea Philippi, which one source tells us was near one of the water sources for the Jordan River.[2]

As we continue Jesus' conversation with His disciples about who He was, we'll notice that He increases the intensity. His disciples had agreed to follow Him, had learned from Him, had even started to live like Him, but there is something He has yet to tell them. Actually, there are two things: one pertaining to Jesus and one pertaining to those who follow Him.

Trading the Known for the Unknown

When we choose to follow Jesus like the disciples, we trade the known of the world for the unknown of life with Christ. And as we all know, trading the known for the unknown is never easy, because it's difficult letting go of our expectations.

Recall a time when your expectations were turned upside down. It may have had to do with how a particular situation unfolded or with information you received. Describe that situation here and how it made you feel:

Jesus drops two proverbial bombs in this conversation. Let's find them together.

1. *The Fate of the Messiah*

We find the first one in Luke 9:22. As He refers to Himself as the Son of Man, Jesus reveals four things that must happen to Him.

Read Luke 9:22, and fill in the blanks below:

1. The Son of Man must _____ many things.

2. The Son of Man must be _____ by the elders, the chief priests, and the teachers of the law.

3. The Son of Man must be _____.

4. On the third day, the Son of Man will be _____ to life.

Imagine the disciples' response to this news! Their beloved Teacher would be killed, likely by the teachers they knew and had respected. Surely this would not be the expected path of Israel's Messiah. And life would come from this? Impossible!

What emotions arise as you reflect on these things that would happen to Jesus?

We've answered this question before in Week 1, but I'll ask it again. What does Jesus' use of the word *must* in these verses tell us about His commitment to pursuing God's will?

This question is purely hypothetical, but what do you think would have happened if Jesus had decided *not* to follow God's plan? List all possible scenarios that you can think of.

Extra Insight

Later in Luke's Gospel we will meet the Sanhedrin, a Jewish governing body that will be responsible for the mock trials resulting in Jesus' death sentence. The Sanhedrin is comprised of the three groups mentioned in Luke 9:22—the elders, the chief priests, and the teachers of the law."[3]

2. The Fate of His Followers

The second proverbial bomb Jesus delivers is found in Luke 9:23, where He reveals three requirements to true discipleship.

Read Luke 9:23 and complete the statements below:

1. A disciple must _____ herself/himself.

2. A disciple must take up her/his _____.

3. A disciple must _____ Jesus.

Here the burden of what Jesus is saying gets heavier. Jesus' followers will suffer also.

Consider the requirement that a disciple must deny herself, and list one to three examples of self-denial that are happening now in your own life or the life of someone you love.

1.

2.

3.

How would you define this requirement in your own words?

To deny yourself means . . .

Jesus would not be the only one to carry a cross. His disciples would have to do this also. Some of them would face a literal death for their obedience; others would face it figuratively.

Can you recall a time when you have felt like you were carrying a figurative cross? If so, describe it here:

How does the addition of the word *daily* influence your understanding of the command to "take up your cross"?

The last requirement is that a disciple must follow Jesus. Based on what we have learned so far about living like Jesus in every moment, what might following Jesus look like in...

how you relate with God?

how you relate with others?

how you relate with yourself?

The Good News

Self-denial and suffering are not things we're eager to sign up for, but there's good news.

Rewrite Luke 9:24 word for word here:

This is the good news, sister. It's probably not what we expected as followers of Jesus, but there is joyous, glorious good news in these words. One writer says it like this:

For Jesus, physical life subject to the dominion of evil is no life at all. It only makes sense to spend one's physical life in such a way as to guarantee eternal, spiritual life in the kingdom of God.[4]

Do you agree or disagree with the statement above? Why?

The New Testament gives us many verses illustrating Jesus' words. Let's examine two of them together.

Read Acts 20:24 and Galatians 2:20 in the margin, and rewrite each verse in your own words below:

Acts 20:24

Galatians 2:20

What expectations do you have about your own life? Dreams, goals, aspirations—lay them all out here:

James 1:17 tells us that every good and perfect gift is from above. All that we have has been showered upon us from heaven. But if Jesus asked you to give it all up today, how hard would that choice be for you? It's okay to be brutally honest here. Jesus knows your heart, and remember that He also understands what it feels like to be human.

Jesus might ask us to forfeit the tangible things of our lives today for the good of His kingdom. He might even ask of us our earthly lives. But regardless of the sacrifices we make as followers of Jesus, the joy of tomorrow is coming.

Read Luke 9:26. What is the good news tucked within this verse? As followers of Jesus, what do we have to look forward to?

Now read Daniel 7:13-14 in the margin. What similarities do you find to Luke 9:26?

This is the good news of what is to come! We can willingly trade the known of this world for the unknown of life with Christ because we know how this all ends: with Jesus on the throne, crowned in glory; with His kingdom never ending; and with us there beside Him. Whatever we face in this life will never compare to the joy of what is waiting for us!

I consider my life worth nothing to me; my only aim is to finish the race and complete the task the Lord Jesus has given me—the task of testifying to the good news of God's grace.
(Acts 20:24)

I have been crucified with Christ and I no longer live, but Christ lives in me. The life I now live in the body, I live by faith in the Son of God, who loved me and gave himself for me.
(Galatians 2:20)

[13]"In my vision at night I looked, and there before me was one like a son of man, coming with the clouds of heaven. He approached the Ancient of Days and was led into his presence. [14]He was given authority, glory and sovereign power; all nations and peoples of every language worshiped him. His dominion is an everlasting dominion that will not pass away, and his kingdom is one that will never be destroyed.
(Daniel 7:13-14)

Trading Expectations for Abundant Life

That's all well and good, you may be thinking, *but what about right now*? You may be wondering what I've wondered at times myself: While we're waiting on the coming Kingdom, how can we live with joy now when life before us fails to meet our expectations?

How do we rejoice when we are standing by a graveside? When we receive the diagnosis? When we lose our job? When the pregnancy test is negative again? When a relationship or marriage is falling apart? When it's easier to reach for a bottle than a dusty Bible? Often this is the way, isn't it? We're taken by surprise when we choose to follow Jesus and bad things still happen.

Why, Jesus? we ask.

I won't know until I ask Him myself, but I would not be surprised if these two words are the most common utterings in heart-wrenching prayers lifted up from this broken world.

When we are whispering such prayers, it can be tempting to attach our expectations of life to the authenticity of God's love. When good things happen, we assume that we hold God's favor; and when bad things happen, we fear we have lost it. But the Bible rejects this lie every time. God's Word reveals that He created us, He loves and values us, and He sustains us. His love is constant and unchanging. Yet Jesus' words from our reading in Luke 9 teach us that every moment wasted on unmet expectations is a moment devoid of real living.

In C. S. Lewis's novel *Till We Have Faces*, the main character, Orual, battles with continued loss and unmet expectations. She says of her journey, "But when the craving went, nearly all that I called myself went with it. It is as if my whole soul had been one tooth and now that tooth was drawn. I was a gap…I know now, Lord, why you utter no answer. You are yourself the answer. Before your face questions die away. What other answer could suffice?"[5]

When we struggle with the question of why, we can remember that the answer is not an explanation. It's a person. A Savior. A King. A Friend. When we surrender our present expectations for future glory with Jesus, He rewards us with abundant, eternal life that begins now. On either side of heaven, the answer is always Jesus. The only way to fully live is to release your expectations for life and instead wait expectantly for Jesus to satisfy.

I don't want to miss what Jesus has planned for me because I was wasting my moments expecting something else. Make no mistake: to live like Jesus will require uncompromising obedience. But the blessing in return is abundant life. Let's be determined to embrace it!

Close today by penning a prayer of surrender to Jesus. Take your time and release your expectations to Him, trusting that He holds them with tender hands. Write your prayer in the margin.

DAY 3: TRANSFORMING OUR FUTURE

I recently shared some of today's lesson with a group of college counselors. They were embarking on two months of work at a summer camp for kids. It would undeniably be one of the best summers of their lives: abundant sunshine, fields of green all around, two giant lakes with every water sport imaginable, laughter, games, late-night ice cream. What's not to love?

It would also be one of the hardest summers of their lives. I know because I worked there as a counselor too. I met my husband while working there, and we remember well the challenges that came with children's camping ministry. With its mission to create the most enjoyable atmosphere possible while making Christ known, Camp Oak Hill brings a number of children to know Jesus as Savior every summer.

When you are making Christ known, however, challenges abound. Some of them will be purely logistical, happenstances that just don't work in your favor. Others will be from unseen spiritual forces as the enemy works hard to deter your progress. And still others will be from the obstacles of moving through a broken world that cannot see past its pain. The love of Christ is not always received with welcoming arms, although the love of Christ is exactly what this world needs most.

The answer to facing these challenges is what we are studying today. We are about to learn how to set our faces like flint.

Read Luke 9:51-62, and put a placeholder there for future reference.

The Quick Three
What happened?
Where did it happen?
What characters are mentioned in this reading?

Setting the Scene

If there is a section of Luke that you will remember above all the others we're studying, I hope it will be this one. This passage marks a turning point in Jesus' ministry, and the motivation He displays is critical to our understanding of determined living.

Up to this point, Jesus has kept His ministry actions in Galilee. But now He changes course to Jerusalem. Along the way, He will travel to Samaria. When traveling through the area, most Jews would go out of their way to avoid Samaria. The Samaritans were descendants of mixed marriages between Jews and Gentiles during an earlier period of Israel's history.[1] To the Jews, the Samaritan people were contaminated with Gentile blood and impure religious traditions. Enemies. But not to Jesus. He has His mind set on a mission that includes the entire world.

Setting Our Faces Like Flint

Our actions are determined by our mind-set. Setting the mind requires focus, intention, and an unwavering effort to sift what does and does not matter. The physical act of putting one foot in front of the other follows the mental act of prioritizing the most important choices. For Jesus, that meant setting His mind on Jerusalem.

Rewrite Luke 9:51 word for word below:

There is an ample supply of treasured words from the Gospel of Luke. But if we were to choose a key verse for our study, this would be it. I want you to see it in a few different translations.

Read each translation of Luke 9:51 below, taking particular note of how the second half of the verse is written. In the last two translations, circle the word that especially pertains to our study.

As the time approached for him to be taken up to heaven, Jesus resolutely set out for Jerusalem. (NIV)

When the days drew near for him to be taken up, he set his face to go to Jerusalem. (ESV)

It came to pass, when the time was come that he should be received up, he steadfastly set his face to go to Jerusalem. (KJV)

When the days were approaching for His ascension, He was determined to go to Jerusalem. (NASB)

When the days were coming to a close for him to be taken up, he determined to journey to Jerusalem. (CSB)

As one source points out, "The phrase 'He was determined' reflects a colloquialism drawn from the Old Testament: 'I have set my face.'"[2] When hearing that phrase, the people would have remembered certain words of the prophet Isaiah.

Read Isaiah 50:7 in the margin. Which phrase recalls a determined mind-set?

Because the Sovereign LORD helps me,
I will not be disgraced.
Therefore have I set my face like flint,
and I know I will not be put to shame.

(Isaiah 50:7)

Isaiah 50 is a prophecy concerning Jesus, the rejection He faces from His people, and His mind-set to keep going in God's will.[3] The phrase "I *have set my face like flint*" in verse 7 literally means "he stiffened his face."[4]

Why this phrase? Because Isaiah is referencing one of the hardest rocks in all of Palestine. Widely available and known for its strength and durability, flint was a popular choice for weapon-making. It's firm and durable qualities made it an easy metaphor for steadfast determination.[5]

What is an example of someone "stiffening their face" to display a resolute conviction to see something through?

I have a confession to make: sometimes I read the last page of a book before I begin. I know, I know. It's a pretty awful habit for a lover of books. But the reality is that the suspense is often too much to bear, and I'd rather not borrow anxiety. I've got enough of that already! We know how this story ends, but let's take a sneak peek anyway.

Glance ahead to Luke 23. What lies ahead in Jerusalem for Jesus?

One commentary says this of Luke 9:51: "Jesus 'set His face' to go to Jerusalem. He not only determined to make the journey; He resolutely tightened His lips, set His jaw, and fixed His eye on the cross and His resurrection. Every story He told, every miracle he performed, and every conversation in which He engaged, from this point on, had the cross pulsating in the back of His mind."[6]

Jesus came into this world with a mission to fulfill. He is stiffening His face toward His death for the salvation of the world. He knows what awaits Him in Jerusalem. Everything that came before and everything that follows after hinges on the attitude He displays in Luke 9:51. Jesus was determined to die so that we might live.

How does knowing this affect your heart toward Jesus? How does it affect your perception of what He thinks of you?

Reread the last two versions of Luke 9:51 on page 122 once more. What does Luke say is approaching for Jesus, and what about this wording is significant?

Luke purposefully mentions that the time was drawing near for Jesus to ascend, to be taken up to heaven—not to be crucified. Knowing Luke to be a clever and intentional writer and the Bible to be inspired by God Himself, it is doubtful that this wording is accidental. The point wasn't just that Jesus was going to die; it was that He was going to *live*—and give us life in the process. This isn't about dying. It's about living abundantly, with Jesus as our guide!

Let's take another sneak peek at the very end of the story, when Jesus does, in fact, ascend to heaven.

Read Luke 24:51-53. What is the response of the people around Jesus?

Determined living is about finding joy in Jesus. It's about setting our faces like flint, stiffening ourselves toward the challenges that lie ahead while softening our hearts toward the hope that is found in Jesus. This is how we live like our Savior!

What lies ahead for you that will need an extra dose of determination to see it through?

Jesus will walk through Samaria on His way to Jerusalem. He will face rejection there also, but He does it anyway. His mission includes the entire world, even when the world doesn't welcome Him. No amount of stereotypical discrimination can keep Him from pursuing the Samaritans. He will not ignore them to please the masses. He will not ignore them to save face. He remains laser-focused on His God-given assignment to bring salvation to the world. Nothing can deter Him, because He refuses to be anything other than determined.

Messengers of Hope

There is a paradox within the Christian faith that we've studied intently this week: true followers of Jesus will face suffering, but living like Jesus will bring hope.

I really appreciate the way my small group leader, Drew Williams, interprets this passage:

> We need to live every day with our heart set on Jerusalem and our mind set on the Ascension.

Let's not forget that there is good news on the way. Jesus knew He would face unspeakable suffering in Jerusalem, and He knew that what awaited Him afterward was unfathomable glory. If we want to truly live the way Jesus intends for us to live, we'll have to determine to look beyond the suffering and hardship we face as believers. The world's hope is at stake.

This is a turning point for Jesus' ministry, and it should be a turning point for us as well. If we choose to be determined now, Jesus will use us to deliver His good news to those who need it most. Determining to live like Jesus will transform us into messengers of hope in a dark and broken world.

Consider what you are setting your face like flint for today. How might what you are facing serve a greater purpose for God's kingdom?

I want to close our day with one insight regarding this unbreakable piece of rock we are wanting to mimic. For years my husband has taken high school students into the mountain wilderness to hike, seek God's beauty in nature, and learn to rely on Him and one another for strength. In his camping bag is a small tool he uses to start a fire from nothing. It's made of flint.

Flint was used in Bible times to make weapons and protect horses' hooves, but it was also used to spark a fire.[7] Not unlike the early church movement that followed Jesus' ascension to heaven, one spark can fan an unending flame. One determined Savior changed the course of the entire world. As His followers, we must continue to fan the flame of His story.

The world around you needs to know that Jesus is determined to love them. Set your face like flint. There is hope to be delivered.

Determining to live like Jesus will transform us into messengers of hope in a dark and broken world.

Extra Insight

Other examples of flint in the Bible can be found in Exodus 4:25; Joshua 5:2; Isaiah 5:28; and Ezekiel 3:9.

DAY 4: REFINING OUR COMFORT ZONES

It was late August, three years ago. My son was near his sixth week of third grade, and I was organizing snacks in the kitchen. Every morning I prayed these words with him on the way to school: "Let us be a family that steps boldly in the name of Jesus."

But this morning I wondered: Have I done this? Have I stepped boldly? Have I lived fearless with you, Jesus? For you?

No. The answer to all these questions was no.

I asked myself if I had just been living in the boat, manning the oars, content to watch others around me walk above the deep? Had I lived safely in my comfort zone, content to worship Him without considering that I am my brother's and sister's keeper, after all? Had I withheld the hope of the gospel from those who needed it most, foolishly thinking that the God stuff in my life was meant for my heart alone? Had I believed the lie that I had nothing to offer?

Yes. The answer to all of these questions was yes.

As I portioned goldfish into the baggies, I asked where I would have to take my faith in order to completely let go of any fears, any hesitations, any doubts.

The resounding answer came from above and within: anywhere except what feels comfortable.

It's our human nature to seek comfort. We like to do what's comfortable; that's why they call it a "comfort zone." But as we will see today, Jesus calls us out of our comfort zones.

Read Luke 10:25-37, and put a placeholder there for future reference.

The Quick Three
What happened?
Where did it happen?
What characters are mentioned in this reading?

Setting the Scene

After a private conversation with His disciples, Jesus' conversation turns public. The initiator? A teacher of the law, which likely implies that he was well educated and professionally trained.[1]

Most of Jesus' conversations with religious leaders spark debate, but this one is relayed without much negativity, despite the fact that the teacher intended to "test Jesus" with his question. Jesus' reply demands that His observers consider the dynamics between Jews and Samaritans, so we will do the same.

Yesterday we received a brief introduction to why the Samaritans were not held in high regard among the Jews. Here is a little more insight into Samaritan history:

> After the people of Judah were exiled to Babylon [606–587 BC] and later returned under the leadership of Ezra and Nehemiah, they found the northern region inhabited by Samaritans, people of mixed Hebrew and Gentile heritage. By then, the returning people of Judah had become known as Jews. Tensions mounted when the Samaritans opposed the rebuilding of Jerusalem and the temple; and the final breach occurred when the Samaritans built their own temple on Mount Gerizim, claiming it, not Jerusalem, to be the authentic place of worship.[2]

Knowing the stereotypes that had developed from this complex history, Jesus answers a question that would be on the minds of his listeners. The answer was not what they would have expected.

Looking for Loopholes

Whether or not you're familiar with Jesus' parable, you've likely heard the term *good Samaritan* in everyday speech.

Considering the modern perception of this phrase, circle any terms below that would describe a good Samaritan today. Feel free to write additional phrases that might not be included here.

a good person   someone who helps others

a selfless person   a compassionate person

someone who supports the poor   someone who helps strangers

others:

All of these answers would be accurate for a modern definition of that phrase, but they wouldn't reflect the entire biblical definition. Let's discover why together.

What question does the law expert ask Jesus in Luke 10:25?

Extra Insight

In keeping with ancient tradition, some Jews today wear phylacteries upon their heads during morning prayers. Within these small boxes are replicas of the Shema, a literal observation of the command in Deuteronomy 6:8:

"Tie them [God's commandments] as symbols on your hands and bind them on your foreheads."[4]

Ever the teacher, Jesus answers the question with another question. Essentially, He asks the law expert about what the law says, leading him to name the central command to the Jewish faith, otherwise known as the Shema, which is found in Deuteronomy 6:4-5.[3] The law expert responds accurately, and also includes the additional command from Leviticus 19:18.

How does the law expert summarize these two commands in Luke 10:27?

Jesus commends the expert for knowing the law so well and encourages him to go live it out, but the conversation doesn't end there. Much like the law expert, this is the part of the passage where I start to raise my hand.

What does the expert ask of Jesus in Luke 10:29?

And the hand is raised. *Wait a minute, Jesus. Who exactly is my neighbor?* The woman on the street corner begging for money? Is she my neighbor? What about the family that lives on the other side of town? The employee at my son's school who speaks a different language? The colleague at work who is covered in tattoos and piercings? My literal next-door neighbor who has a different skin color than me? Are these all my neighbors?

Jesus answers with a Samaritan story.

Describe what happens in Luke 10:30.

The scenario Jesus has pictured was a very real threat. When traveling from Galilee to Judea, Jews would typically take a path that circumvented Samaria; but it left them vulnerable to attacks from thieves and vagabonds along the journey, which is why this path was often referred to as "the bloody way."[5]

Three people respond to the battered traveler in verses 31-35. List who they are and how they respond by completing the chart:

	Who is this person?	How do they respond?
First Responder		

	Who is this person?	How do they respond?
Second Responder		
Third Responder		

It is possible that both the priest and the Levite were concerned with the risk of ritual impurity by touching a seemingly dead body (see Numbers 19:11 in the margin). But Jesus implies that they were simply looking for loopholes in the command to love their neighbor as themselves.

Whoever touches a human corpse will be unclean for seven days.

(Numbers 19:11)

Do you ever find yourself looking for loopholes in what God has commanded you? If so, list an example here:

In the Old Testament law, there's evidence to suggest that the command to love one's neighbor envisioned only, at least primarily, their fellow Israelites (see Leviticus 19:17-18, which mentions "neighbor" alongside "fellow Israelite" and "your people"). So their neighbor was often their fellow worshiper of Yahweh, the one true God. While there may have been ethical, cultural, and social differences among them, these differences would have been much less pronounced than with other peoples or nations. It's easier to love your neighbor when your neighbor looks like you.

But Jesus affirms that God calls us to understand this command more broadly. With the proclamation of a new kingdom, Jesus emphasizes God's radically inclusive standards.

Given the history between Jews and Samaritans, why would the Samaritan's actions have been considered radical?

The Samaritan wasn't just a good person. The Samaritan was a good person who went outside of his comfort zone to love others. His actions were radical because he showed thoughtful and thorough mercy to a perceived enemy that allowed the traveler to be fully restored. Not only did he tenderly care for his wounds but he also tangibly provided a way for him to heal.

Can you think of a specific situation where this lesson from the Samaritan could be applied in your neighborhood, city, or state?

Stepping out of your comfort zone to love others is where Jesus wants you and me to be. When you do, you might find yourself walking a path that feels easy and light. But what if you don't? What if the road you're walking on isn't well worn or easy to travel? What if no one has ever traveled it before at all?

You're not alone. I've been around long enough to notice that God rarely calls us to places of comfort when He is leading us to our calling. But we can remember that Jesus has shown you and me the same mercy that the Samaritan gave to the weary traveler. At one point, we were outsiders to the kingdom of God. Battered and broken, Jesus cared for our wounds and made a way for the restoration and redemption of our souls. I wonder if He is echoing the words of the Samaritan in Luke 10:35 to us today?

Insert your name in the blank below as you imagine Jesus saying this to you today:

_____ , I'm entrusting the people of this world to your care. They might not look like you, talk like you, think like you, or act like you, but they are hurting and in need of rest and healing. You know how good it feels to be loved by Me. Show them this in your actions, and then teach them what you know of Me. I'm giving you my Word and all the provisions you will need to care for them. Look after them. When I return, I will reward you for your obedience. Remember mercy. Remember Me. Remember to love your neighbor.

Stepping Out of Our Comfort Zones

One of my dearest friends works for a charitable aid organization that I like to support, The Preemptive Love Coalition. Their mission is to restore violence-induced loss by providing relief to communities that would stereotypically be considered enemies. They aren't looking for loopholes. They're jumping over walls to actively pursue war-torn communities and displaced refugees. They meet urgent physical needs but don't stop there. They create jobs for victims, actively engage in peacemaking strategies, and provide local solutions to local problems. Although they are not an overtly faith-based organization, one of their core value statements reads as if it is drawn straight from the pages of Luke 10:

"We exist to go where no one else will go, to love the people no one else will love."[6]

A dangerous undercurrent runs beneath the tensions of humanity, whispering that our worth is determined by the actions and opinions of our fellow humans. But the truth is that your worth is determined by the God who created you, the One who knew your life before you were even in your mother's womb, the One who set you in this very time and place for a reason, and the One who made you in His image. First, we need to convince our own hearts that our worth is defined by God, not our neighbor. And then we need to pursue our neighbor.

It will take courage to step outside of our comfort zones. But we should do it because of one simple reason: Jesus said so.

This is the only way we as humans will fight the lie that if our neighbor says so, then we don't matter. As your neighbor, I have the responsibility and privilege to tell you that your well-being is important because it's important to Jesus. Racism, sexism, classism—every discrimination that exists—will fall to the truths of Luke 10. But it won't happen unless we're willing to leave what is comfortable. Wholehearted devotion to Jesus prompts us to leave our comfort zones to love our neighbor.

> Close today by asking Jesus the question from Luke 10:29: *Jesus, who is my neighbor?* Ask Him to open your eyes to those in your community who don't look like you, don't talk like you, don't think like you, and don't act like you. Then ask Him to reveal tangible ways that you can step out of your comfort zones to love them. Make some notes in the margin.

Determine to be not just a good Samaritan, but a radical one!

DAY 5: ALIGNING OUR HEARTS

Every day we are faced with decisions. From the insignificant to the impactful, our lives can be summed up with a series of choices. One foot in front of the other, to the left or to the right, sometimes forward and sometimes back—within each choice lies two outcomes: one step closer to Jesus or one step away from Him.

A stagnant existence does not exist. We are changed by the choices we make.

We live in a culture that is defined more clearly by distraction than intent. We are at no loss for options to escape the reality that marches ahead of us. But when we make one unintentional choice after another, the passing of time quickly becomes a vapor instead of a memory made. Fun? Maybe. Satisfying? Never.

Wholehearted devotion to God prompts us to leave our comfort zones to love our neighbor.

What you and I are learning together is that this doesn't even remotely qualify as what Jesus intended when He said *follow me, I know the way to abundant life!* What He intended for us was a life lived to the fullest; but if we're not careful, we'll spend our lives wandering around in a proverbial wilderness of distraction instead of experiencing a full, rewarding, and worthwhile life here on earth.

That is, unless we determine to make another choice. There is another way, and Jesus will use someone who oozes discipleship to teach it to us. Only this time, we'll learn from a woman.

Read Luke 10:38-42, and put a placeholder there for future reference.

The Quick Three
What happened?
Where did it happen?
What characters are mentioned in this reading?

Setting the Scene

Just in case we haven't noticed, let's begin today by recognizing how radical Jesus was. The words He said, the actions He took, the standards of belief He introduced, the people He chose to spend time with—all were radical in His day and culture. I can imagine a chorus of dropped jaws and wide eyes following wherever He went, not to mention both the overt displays of revolt against Him that we have already studied and the subversive plans mounting against Him. To the shock of observers all around, Jesus routinely challenged religious and cultural norms.

Today would be no different.

Luke has already told us of women who were supporting Jesus' ministry out of their own means (Luke 8:1-3). Today we will see a woman in a role that was traditionally reserved for men. Although Luke doesn't tell us the specific location, John 11:1 reveals that we are in Bethany, a village just outside of Jerusalem. Jesus is getting closer to His target, but not before He sees someone who can't wait to sit at His feet.

Let's do a personal assessment. Whether or not you are familiar with the story of Mary and Martha, you're likely familiar with their dominant traits. We'll call them the doer and the learner. If you were labeling yourself with one of these traits today, which one would you choose?

What does Luke 10:40 tell us about how Martha responded to Mary's behavior?

In defense of all the Marthas out there, I need to affirm that this world needs *doers*. I am not one of them. My husband is. I'm rather prone to getting lost in whatever I'm engaged in at the moment. He prefers to have a list and get things done. Together we make a wonderful team. In our task-driven society, it's easy to assume that Martha's response is driven by the hospitality chores that have now been dumped on her.

But pull the twenty-first-century veil off your eyes and consider the cultural norms of Jesus' day. R. T. France notes that women were not typically seen in a discipleship role then. They did not have the privilege of learning from Master Teachers. Is it possible that Martha was just as shocked by seeing her sister at Jesus' feet as she was at not receiving adequate help?[1]

How does Jesus respond to Martha's outcry in verses 41-42?

Remember, Jesus is radical, and He's introducing a new way with God's kingdom. Martha still may be accustomed to the old. How does Jesus' response to her affect your sense of fairness?

Why is Mary's choice the better one?

True to his priority of showcasing the marginalized as worthy of a significant place in God's kingdom, Luke portrays Mary as a true disciple. The reason that her choice was a better one has more to do with the priorities of her heart than the work of her hands. Martha's commitment to hospitality was not the wrong choice, but Mary's choice prompts us to consider how well we apply Jesus' command to discipleship.

Which characteristics of true discipleship do you see evident in Mary in this passage?

I've listed some, but not all, of the qualities of true followers of Jesus that we have studied so far. Take a moment and flip back through your workbook to add any others that have resonated with you:

___ Pursuit of wisdom	Others:
___ Obedience	___ _____
___ Denying self	___ _____
___ Friend of sinners	___ _____
___ Sharing the good news of Christ	___ _____
___ Prayer	___ _____

Now, rank each of the above qualities as follows:
1 – I am excelling in this area of discipleship
2 – I am proficient in this area of discipleship, but there is always room for growth
3 – I need help in deepening my commitment to this area of discipleship

The goal of this exercise isn't to identify weaknesses but to recognize areas where we can ask Jesus for help. Having a Mary heart in a world full of distractions will require our intentions to originate from within. Nothing will stick if our convictions about following Jesus aren't flowing directly from the heart. To help us do that, we're going to enlist the power of God's Word.

Choose three verses below to read and meditate on. Rewrite each verse you chose in your own words to the right.

Proverbs 4:23

Psalm 51:10

Psalm 112:7

1 Timothy 1:5

James 4:8

Luke 10:27

Glance at your ranked list above, and note any qualities you ranked as a two or three. Using the verses you chose to meditate on, take a few moments to pray over each of these discipleship qualities, asking Jesus to give you wisdom and direction in deepening your heart toward His.

I'll give you an example: Jesus, your Word in Psalm 51:10 promises that you will purify my heart and renew my spirit. Would you purify and burden my heart for prayer and give me steadfast determination to grow this area in my life?

Choosing Life

I don't think Mary and Martha were all that different. I just think that Mary may have had a better grasp on the motivational source for true servanthood. Every day we are called to serve the kingdom of God. There is work to do to bring hope into the world. But works performed without devotion will only lead to resentment. On the other hand, service that overflows from sitting at Jesus' feet gives us peace that our choices will always be the right ones. When our hearts are fully connected to Jesus, we are better equipped to serve others.

I met Jill Savage, a Christian author and speaker, at a writing conference a few years back. There she shared her wisdom on intentional living based on Deuteronomy 30:19-20. It's a passage that is dear to my heart because it is what motivated me to get out of bed after my diagnosis of Vascular Ehlers-Danlos Syndrome. Still reeling from the ramifications of the diagnosis, I was ill-equipped to serve my family well until God graciously brought me to this passage:

> [19]*I call heaven and earth to witness against you today, that I have set before you life and death, blessing and curse. Therefore choose life, that you and your offspring may live,* [20]*loving the* LORD *your God, obeying his voice and holding fast to him, for he is your life and length of days, that you may dwell in the land that the* LORD *swore to your fathers, to Abraham, to Isaac, and to Jacob, to give them.*
>
> (Deuteronomy 30:19-20 ESV)

I keep the following list from Jill's teaching (the bolded words below)[2] hanging in my office as a reminder of the practical daily choices we can make to live effectively for God. All of them stem from a heart that is aligned with Jesus. As we close today, I leave this list with you because I think Mary would have made these choices also, and I know Jesus would approve. What follows each grouping of bolded words is my paraphrase of Jill's teaching.

7 PRACTICAL WAYS TO CHOOSE LIFE EVERY DAY

1. **Choose people over projects**. God calls us to love the person right in front of us. This could be your child, your family member or loved one, or your coworker. Pay attention to where God is

> When our hearts are fully connected to Jesus, we are better equipped to serve others.

One author notes that it's important to recognize that Luke inserts this story just after Jesus' teaching on the importance of serving others. That's not accidental, but it is intentional as Luke wants his readers to remember that only by prioritizing our devotion to Jesus will we be able to love others well.[3]

sending you on this day, and love the people He places in your path.

2. **Choose God over goals**. We may have to grieve the loss of our dream to make room for where God wants us to go. He has plans for us. If He opens a door you don't have on your radar screen, be prepared to adjust and trust that His plans for you are good.

3. **Choose margin over mayhem**. The moments in our lives where we can retreat from the world and listen to God speak are our margins. Silence is where God gives us our marching orders. We need margin to create, to live effectively, and to handle whatever comes our way.

4. **Choose mission over money**. Whatever God is calling you to do, do it because it's a part of who God made you to be.

5. **Choose perfected over perfect**. We have a tendency to compare our insides to other's outsides. Change the story you see in your head when you look at someone else; she has a back story that you don't know. There is no perfect, but God is perfecting us every day.

6. **Choose calling over counting**. Your story is powerful, and the human experience is far more important than any tools you may use to rate your worth. Let God do the counting while you pursue your calling.

7. **Choose love over lists**. Compassion for others has to rule everything we do, and it must be at the top of every one of our to-do lists.

As we move forward, let's determine to make these choices every day to ensure both our hearts and our actions are in tune with Jesus. They are guaranteed to lead us along the path to abundant living with Him.

Luke 9:51-56

Jesus was determined to _____ you.

Becoming farsighted in our faith will strengthen our nearsighted
_____.

The choice to live like Jesus will require _____, but it will also be
steeped in _____.

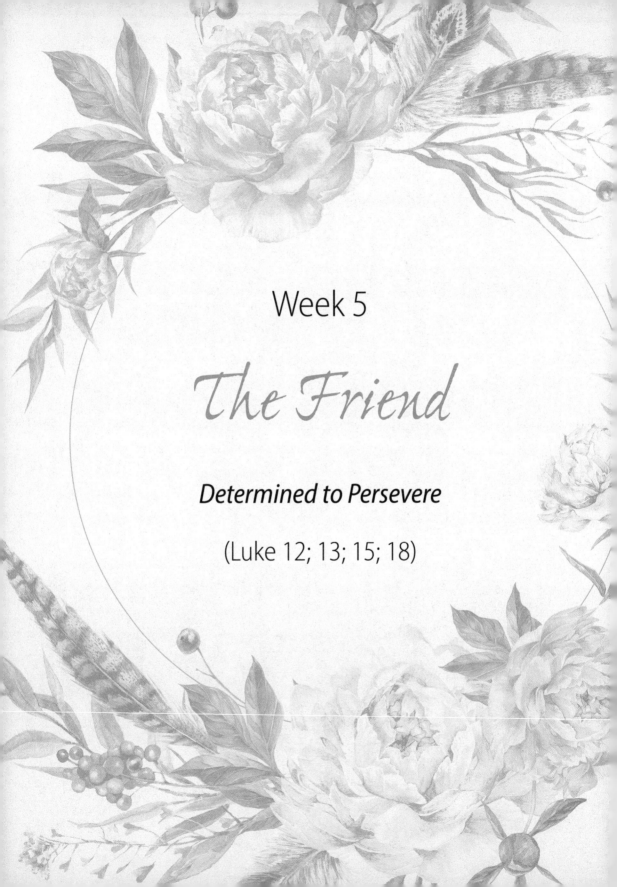

Week 5

The Friend

Determined to Persevere

(Luke 12; 13; 15; 18)

> Blessed is the one who perseveres under trial because,
> having stood the test, that person will receive the crown
> of life that the Lord has promised to those who love him.
>
> (James 1:12)

I recently watched a video clip with tears streaming down my face. I was not hormonal, and it wasn't a promo for a Hallmark movie. It was a clip of three marathon runners, approaching the end of a race.

One runner was in the lead, but his legs were faltering. I'm not a runner myself, so I can only guess at the physical endurance required to complete such a race. But it was clear that this runner was not experiencing normal fatigue. He was very near the verge of passing out. Losing his sense of direction and his ability to control his legs, my heart dropped as I watched him give up the lead he had kept for the last quarter of the race.

The runner behind him passed without a second glance at his collapsing posture.

Then from around the corner the third runner appeared. Without breaking his pace, he wrapped his arms around the first runner's shoulders and continued the race with the first runner right next to him. Feet matched feet. Legs matched legs. Together they determined to reach the finish line.

Already there was the second runner who had kept on going. He looked triumphant as he broke through the winner's ribbon.

Just beyond were the two determined ones, still together—the one runner still supporting the other. As they approached the finish line, the third runner released his weakened companion, but not before giving him a powerful shove to make sure he crossed the finish line first.[1] I *sobbed*. It still brings me to tears as I'm retelling it now.

I listened to the commentators just after the race to learn that the two runners who had reached the finish line together were brothers. *Best friends*. The younger was the one who had faltered, and the older was the one who had saved him. More tears.

Whatever we are facing as we head into this week of study together, Jesus is facing it with us as our closest friend. I used to think that accepting Christ as your Savior simply meant that your sins were forgiven and Jesus would one day welcome you into heaven. I didn't realize until later that He also longs to welcome me as a friend. When we are tired, when we are weary, or when we need someone to carry us and shove us across the finish line, we can call on Jesus.

He will always be working with our best interests in mind.

DAY 1: READY TO LIVE

In early 2018, a South African palliative care doctor interviewed his terminally ill patients on the meaning of life and the things that give it the most value. The heartbreaking beauty behind the responses is that they were all from children ages four to nine. Dr. McAlpine is a pediatrician.

What brought his young patients the most joy were things like snuggling with their pets, making memories at the beach, reading and being told stories, playing with their toys, and of course, ice cream. Laughter and kindness were named as highly valued character traits, and at the top of their list of treasures was time with family and friends. No one wished for more hours in front of the television or increased exposure to social media.

Dr. McAlpine summed up his interviews this way: "Take home message: Be kind. Read more books. Spend time with your family. Crack jokes. Go to the beach. Hug your dog. Tell that special person you love them. These are the things these kids wished they could've done more. The rest is details. Oh...and eat ice-cream."[1]

With the clarity of an innocent mind, these children recognized something that usually takes years for most adults to realize: awareness of life's brevity is a beautiful gift. Our days on earth are precious. Every memory is priceless. Every moment matters.

What do you enjoy most about life, and what brings life the most meaning?

With Jesus, there is another thing we'll want to cling to if we want to embrace the true meaning of life.

Read Luke 12:13-21, and put a placeholder there for future reference.

The Quick Three
What happened?
Where did it happen?
What characters are mentioned in this reading?

Setting the Scene

Tensions are rising as we near Jerusalem. Our reading plan has taken us through Luke 11, which details some of the growing opposition toward Jesus. As R. T. France points out, we'll see that Jesus shifts His focus toward the emphasis of spiritual matters over material assets as He gets closer to the cross and the coming kingdom of God.[2] Today's reading launches us into that shift.

At the heart of this passage is a discussion on matters of inheritance, although the conversation undoubtedly didn't go in the direction that the man from the crowd intended. Rabbis often handled legal disputes,[3] so it seems the man hoped Jesus would solve his dilemma.

Jesus had a greater lesson in mind that He wanted to make clear. And to get to that lesson, we need to explore the laws of inheritance.

Laws of Inheritance

In Luke 12, we see that a large crowd has gathered, and Jesus is teaching them (vv. 1-12). Suddenly someone calls out from the crowd.

What does the man from the crowd ask Jesus to do in Luke 12:13?

We don't know if the man from the crowd is an older or younger brother, but we can assume that he is the younger based on what we know of Jewish law.

There are three types of biblical inheritance we'll consider today. Let's start with the one this man is most concerned with.

1. *Inheritance Received from Parents*

Read the following Old Testament passages, and note the laws of inheritance described in each:

Deuteronomy 21:15-17

Numbers 27:8

Numbers 27:9-11

Of the three laws of inheritance above, which one do you think the man from the crowd took objection to?

Why do you think Jesus refused to arbitrate between the brothers, as we read in Luke 12:14?

2. Land Inheritance Received from God

Old Testament inheritance also included the land given by God to the children of Israel.

What does Deuteronomy 11:8-9 tell us about the land promised to the Jewish nation?

Essentially, what piece of advice does Jesus give the crowd in Luke 12:15?

Using one of His favorite ways to teach, Jesus explains His advice with a parable.

Reread the story of the rich fool below, circling every instance where the rich man refers to himself (look for *I* and *my*):

¹⁶*He told them this parable: "The ground of a certain rich man yielded an abundant harvest. ¹⁷He thought to himself, 'What shall I do? I have no place to store my crops.'*

¹⁸*"Then he said, 'This is what I'll do. I will tear down my barns and build bigger ones, and there I will store my surplus grain. ¹⁹And I'll say to myself, "You have plenty of grain laid up for many years. Take life easy; eat, drink and be merry."'*

²⁰*"But God said to him, 'You fool! This very night your life will be demanded from you. Then who will get what you have prepared for yourself?'*

²¹*"This is how it will be with whoever stores up things for themselves but is not rich toward God."*

(Luke 12:16-21)

Jesus isn't denouncing material possessions. He is making a point about priorities.

What are the priorities of the rich man in this parable?

This parable is known as *The Parable of the Rich Fool*. Why do you think the man is labeled as a fool?

As I've mentioned, I lost my mother at a young age. The loss of a parent at any time is not without arduous challenges as you learn to walk through life without what should be your most formative and influential relationship. Because I was still a child when my mother left this earth, I grew in ways that my peers would not experience until much later in life. But what I lost in innocence, I gained in perspective. Although the weight of death hung heavy in my mind, it also helped me identify what was most important in life. I have not always welcomed that perspective, but I do recognize how it positively shaped some of the choices I've made. If you've walked a similar path, you also know it to be a hard-won gift—but a gift nonetheless. When you've lost what matters most, you are quicker to notice the things that truly matter.

In Luke 12, Jesus proposes another way to embrace valuable perspective. We don't have to look very far to find it: our greatest treasures lie in our spiritual wealth. This is the third type of biblical inheritance.

3. *Spiritual Inheritance Shared with Christ*

Unlike the other two biblical inheritance laws, this one applies to all believers, including you and me. Because of Jesus, we all share a spiritual inheritance.

What do the following passages tell us about our spiritual family identity?

Romans 8:16-17

Colossians 1:12

Colossians 3:24

Hebrews 9:15

God so loved the world that he gave his one and only Son, that whoever believes in him shall not perish but have eternal life.

(John 3:16)

John 3:16 (in the margin) delivers the most important inheritance law for every believer. Those who embrace Jesus Christ as their Savior will receive the inheritance of eternal life. A life lived with Jesus—through His Spirit here on earth and face-to-face in heaven—is our richest treasure.

Take a moment to describe what it feels like to receive this wonderful gift. Write as if you are writing directly to Jesus.

"I have told you these things, so that in me you may have peace. In this world you will have trouble. But take heart! I have overcome the world."

(John 16:33)

We don't have to wait until we get to heaven to tangibly experience some of that treasure. What we are studying together is evidence that a life lived like Jesus is rich with spiritual rewards, even as we walk through a broken world.

What rewards has walking with Jesus brought you

. . . since you asked Him to be your Savior?

. . . during your most difficult season of life?

. . . in the past four weeks of our time together studying Luke?

. . . since you woke up this morning?

¹⁶Therefore we do not lose heart. Though outwardly we are wasting away, yet inwardly we are being renewed day by day. ¹⁷For our light and momentary troubles are achieving for us an eternal glory that far outweighs them all. ¹⁸So we fix our eyes not on what is seen, but on what is unseen, since what is seen is temporary, but what is unseen is eternal.

(2 Corinthians 4:16-18)

The life of a follower of Jesus will undoubtedly bring hardship and suffering. John 16:33 (in the margin) tells us as much. Even so, how have you found that walking with Jesus brings peace and joy?

Read 2 Corinthians 4:16-18 in the margin. What truths from this passage might help you explain the paradox of finding peace and joy in the midst of hardship and suffering to someone who does not know Jesus? What truths from this passage bring *you* hope today?

The richest reward of living like Jesus is that eternity begins when we align our hearts to His. Just as material possessions can never compare to our spiritual riches, neither can earthly hardship outweigh eternal joy. The biggest problem for the man from the crowd in today's reading isn't that he has an inheritance dispute. It is that he doesn't understand the value of the true inheritance that is right in front of him.

An Eternal Perspective

The children from Dr. McAlpine's practice had little trouble embracing abundant life, even though their slice of life was far too short by our expectations. They knew what mattered most: it's people who hold the greatest value. That, and ice cream, and I don't dare disagree with them on that one. They remained ready to live because their perspective was focused on what gives life meaning.

How's your perspective today? Is it focused on the material things that are easily seen or the spiritual truths that we know by faith? Following Jesus brings incomparable value to our lives. Embracing an eternal perspective over temporal satisfaction will make us ready to live life to the fullest.

Never am I more aware of this than in the morning right after I wake up. After a night of letting my subconscious rule, the morning alarm shines a tangible light on the day's troubles.

Oh, I've got to make *that* call today.

How am I going to pay *those* bills?

I don't know how I'm ever going to make *this* decision.

I wish I could take back *those* words that I said.

When my perspective is focused on the temporal, placing two feet on the floor in the morning to start the day can be difficult. But we'll miss out on truly living if we let our minds cling to what is worldly.

On the mornings when we need a perspective shift, we can remember the truth of God's Word to help us move forward. Let's close today by forming a few pep talk statements based on biblical truth. I like to write these on a note card and place it on my nightstand so it is the first thing I see when I wake up. I'll give you a few examples of mine, and then you can add some of your own below.

- Today might bring pain, but Jesus will use it for my good and for the good of His kingdom.
- Today feels like the impossible, but nothing is impossible with Jesus.
- I might face hardship today, but one day I will share in Jesus' glory in heaven.
- What I see today can never compare with what is awaiting me.

> Embracing an eternal perspective over temporal satisfaction will make us ready to live life to the fullest.

Extra Insight

We can mistakenly believe that we are embracing abundant life even when our perspective is focused on the wrong things. But as Jesus is quick to suggest in Luke 12:20, anything other than an eternal perspective leads to death.

Extra Insight

Jesus also uses this parable to expose the pitfalls of coveting worldly possessions,[4] a temptation He would remember well from His forty days in the desert at the beginning of His ministry. First Timothy 6:6-10 offers wise counsel against the love of money.

Put two feet on the floor, sister. Abundant life in Jesus is waiting for you!

DAY 2: FINDING PEACE BY STRAIGHTENING OUR PRIORITIES

The findings of yet another study on stress indicate that the psychological impact of stress can manifest itself physically in the body, leading to sickness, disease, and even death.[1] This is not a shock to us. We live in a culture that breeds anxiety; and each of us either knows someone who has experienced a health concern as a direct result from the effects of stress, or we have encountered this ourselves. From a minor headache to a massive heart attack, stress can contribute to bodily disfunction.

Although we are just pairing scientific evidence with this truth in our day, the dilemma is not new. It applies to the entire human condition throughout time. We are fortunate to live in an era when we have many resources for managing stress, but I'd like to begin today with the words of the One who created the human body. He knows how to help us find peace.

Read Luke 12:22-34, and put a placeholder there for future reference.

The Quick Three
What happened?
Where did it happen?
What characters are mentioned in this reading?

Setting the Scene

Although we are picking up where we left off yesterday, the original language in Luke 12:22 "indicates a change in audience."[2] Luke tells us as much when he mentions that Jesus is now speaking to His disciples, but we can assume that at least a little time has passed between Jesus' conversation with the man from the crowd and this new conversation with His disciples.

Whereas yesterday's reading dealt with an abundance of material possessions, today's reading addresses a lack of them. Knowing Luke and his storytelling finesse, this is likely not coincidental. He knew that Jesus was preparing His disciples for what was to come. And Jesus' wisdom will be useful for us too. Let's dive in.

To Be Made Whole

Look again at Luke 12:22. What did Jesus tell the disciples not to do?

Depending on which version you are reading from, you might have written "do not be anxious" (ESV), "do not worry about your life" (NIV, NASB, CSB), "take no thought for your life" (KJV), or something similar. In the original Greek language, this phrase means "to be torn apart."[3] Our culture may have changed tremendously since these words were originally penned, but the definition of stress and anxiety have not. The effects of stress can leave us feeling completely and utterly torn apart.

Can you think of a time when you felt "torn apart"—when your mind vacillated between the *what ifs* of the future? If so, take a moment to describe it now:

If you are reeling from the effects of stress today, there is a remedy awaiting you in Jesus' words. He understands how you feel. He knows your heart. He knows how easily anxiety can make you feel torn apart. And He knows the way to put everything back together.

Of the things that are currently bringing you the most anxiety, list the top three here:

1.

2.

3.

Now list the concerns that Jesus addresses in Luke 12:22-29:

Would you categorize these concerns as worldly or spiritual, and why?

Read the various renderings of Luke 12:30 below, taking note of the underlined phrase in each:

For the pagan world <u>runs after</u> all such things, and your Father knows that you need them. (NIV, emphasis added)

For all the nations of the world <u>seek after</u> these things, and your Father knows that you need them. (ESV, emphasis added)

For all these things the nations of the world <u>eagerly seek</u>; but your Father knows that you need these things. (NASB, emphasis added)

How would you rewrite these phrases in your own words?

The English word for *priority* did not originate until the mid-fourteenth century[4]; but even so, Jesus is addressing the concept of priorities in this conversation with His disciples. Our priorities determine our peace. The by-product for placing worldly concerns over spiritual ones is worry.

Knowing how easy it is to focus on worldly concerns, Jesus reassures His disciples with God's promises of provision.

Find the promise in each Scripture below, and summarize it in your own words:

Luke 12:24

Luke 12:28

Luke 12:29-30

How is each of the following verses similar to Jesus' teaching in today's reading?

Psalm 34:10

Philippians 4:19

2 Corinthians 9:8

Glance back at your top three concerns that you listed on page 147. How would you classify each concern—worldly or spiritual?

1.

2.

3.

If our priorities determine our peace, how can we redirect the focus of our hearts on godly priorities instead? Jesus answers this question in Luke 12:31.

Read Luke 12:31. Instead of worldly concerns, what does Jesus encourage His disciples to seek?

To seek God's kingdom is to prioritize His will over your desires and reap the benefits of an intimate relationship with Him. Charles Swindoll writes, "Pour your energy, your time, your money, your every earthly resource into God's great kingdom enterprise; and He will adorn you, feed you, console you, and eventually give you unfettered access to all that is His."[5]

What feels torn apart can be made whole if we allow Jesus to realign our priorities.

Setting Our Minds

When my son was a baby, we had a special routine before naptime. A little walk up and down the hallway, a little sway in the rocking chair, a little pat on his back. All the while during these little steps of our routine, I played an a capella version of one of my favorite hymns as he settled for sleep, "His Eye Is on the Sparrow." I love the reassurance in this song that "His eye is on the sparrow, / And I know He watches me."[6] I know that at six months old he was not able to understand those lyrics. But in my wistful mother's mind, I wondered if one day when he was older he might hear that tune again and somehow all the comfort of those precious naptime moments would come right back to him, settling in his heart and reassuring him that he was loved, protected, cared for, and valued.

Realigning our priorities with God's priorities reduces our anxiety.

I hoped that even after years had gone by, that song would trigger a response in him that might soothe his restless heart.

God's Word does this very thing for us. Its truth triggers a memory planted in our DNA—that we are daughters of a King who loves us, protects us, cares for us, and values us. His Word settles our hearts when fear, worry, and anxiety want to take root because it reminds us of God's priorities over ours. Realigning our priorities with God's priorities reduces our anxiety.

In his Letter to the Philippians, the Apostle Paul writes of setting our minds to the priorities of God:

> 8Finally, brothers and sisters, whatever is true, whatever is noble, whatever is right, whatever is pure, whatever is lovely, whatever is admirable—if anything is excellent or praiseworthy—think about such things. 9Whatever you have learned or received or heard from me, or seen in me—put it into practice. And the God of peace will be with you.
>
> (Philippians 4:8-9)

As we close today, let's begin this practice by considering our current stressors in several key areas of life.

> Take a moment now to prayerfully think through anything that is bringing you anxiety in each area. If there is anxiety there, jot down a few words to briefly describe it. Then pray the given verse over the concern that is causing stress.
>
> Relationships:

> 4Love is patient, love is kind. It does not envy, it does not boast, it is not proud. 5It does not dishonor others, it is not self-seeking, it is not easily angered, it keeps no record of wrongs. 6Love does not delight in evil but rejoices with the truth. 7It always protects, always trusts, always hopes, always perseveres.
>
> (1 Corinthians 13:4-7)

> Work:

> Whatever you do, work at it with all your heart, as working for the Lord, not for human masters.
>
> (Colossians 3:23)

Family:

For this reason I kneel before the Father, from whom every family in heaven and on earth derives its name. I pray that out of his glorious riches he may strengthen you with power through his Spirit in your inner being, so that Christ may dwell in your hearts through faith.

(Ephesians 3:14-17a)

Finances:

I was young and now I am old,
yet I have never seen the righteous forsaken
or their children begging bread.
They are always generous and lend freely;
their children will be a blessing.

(Psalm 37:25-26)

Health:

He said to me, "My grace is sufficient for you, for my power is made perfect in weakness." Therefore I will boast all the more gladly about my weaknesses, so that Christ's power may rest on me.

(2 Corinthians 12:9)

Let the truth of His Word wash over every area that brings anxiety. As you continue to bring these concerns to Jesus' feet this week, may He cover you with His abundant peace.

DAY 3: ON BEING STEADFAST

Having lost both her husband and her sister to cancer, Katie Couric offered these words in a 2005 interview: "I'm very interested in exploring a more spiritual side of me, and I'm in the process of doing that, both formally and informally. I really envy those who have a steadfast, unwavering faith, because I think it's probably so comforting and helpful during difficult times."[1]

Extra Insight

As Jesus' disciples heard this conversation, they likely remembered the teachings of the Cynics and Stoics, who taught "detachment from material concerns." But unlike those groups who promoted simplicity for the sake of self-sufficiency, Jesus taught total reliance on God.[7]

I agree that an unwavering faith provides a constant source of comfort. It carries us through hardship and suffering. It sees us through to the other side of sorrow. Paul writes in 2 Corinthians 1:3-4 that we serve "the God of all comfort, who comforts us in all our troubles, so that we can comfort those in any trouble with the comfort we ourselves receive from God."

Faith gives rise to comfort, always. But unwavering faith does more than offer comfort; it provides the motivation to keep going when everything else is telling us to give up.

Faith in Jesus is the answer to every scenario that prompts us to quit. Why? Because quitting was something Jesus never did.

Read Luke 13:31-35, and put a placeholder there for future reference.

The Quick Three
What happened?
Where did it happen?
What characters are mentioned in this reading?

Setting the Scene

Imagine that the worst possible news you could receive would also bring confirmation that you were exactly where you needed to be. I think you'll agree that bad news is unwelcome news. We avoid it at all costs. Most people I know, myself included, generally do whatever it takes *not* to receive troubling news.

Quite the opposite, in our reading today we see that Jesus has done whatever it takes to make sure that He *does* receive the awful news delivered by the Pharisees. Of course, Jesus has known this to be His path all along.

The news that Herod wants to kill Him means that Jesus is walking in God's will for His time on earth. We know that with the cross and the ascension that would follow, His death will actually glorify His heavenly Father and bring great rejoicing in the kingdom of God. However, this doesn't change the fact that the upfront news is bad. Jesus knows He will soon face unspeakable pain and shame on the cross, and He is about to show us what keeps Him steadfast in His mission to defeat it.

A Longing to Gather

Before we dive in, let's think about how we might have felt in Jesus' shoes. Hearing that someone of influence and power wanted us dead would be difficult news to hear. The natural human response would be fear, and we might be tempted to throw in the towel and run or hide. We know what that's like because so often we are tempted to give up in lesser ways.

Think for a moment about a situation in which you wanted to give up. Perhaps it was a situation at work or an issue with family. Did you keep going and finish the task? If so, what kept you from walking away?

Take a look at Luke 13:32. How does Jesus respond to the messenger's warning?

Jesus' goal is Jerusalem, and we've noted before that He was resolute in making His divine appointment there (Luke 9:51).

Read Luke 13:33 in the margin. What phrase in this verse further implies that Jesus is determined to stay the course?

How would you describe the overall tone in Jesus' words in the passage for today?

I'll be quite candid with you. This passage has always been difficult for me to read. It's ominous and foreboding, and Jesus' overall words bring little comfort. But tucked within Luke 13:34 are three words that give me pause.

Refer to Luke 13:34 and complete the following:

"Jerusalem, Jerusalem, you who kill the prophets and stone those sent to you, how often _____ _____ _____
to gather your children together, as a hen gathers her chicks under her wings, and you were not willing."

What does this verse tell us about the character of Jesus?

Extra Insight

By calling Herod Antipas a fox, Jesus was not implying that he was smart and cunning but that he was "without honor, perhaps also with the implication of being devious."[2]

In any case, I must press on today and tomorrow and the next day—for surely no prophet can die outside Jerusalem!
(Luke 13:33)

"I have longed." Despite the dreaded warning from the Pharisee and the fact that most of Jesus' words are measured and full of lament, these three words give me hope because they reveal His tender heart for humanity. Even when the world is rebelling against Him, Jesus remains protectively compassionate toward humanity.

In the Book of Lamentations, the prophet Jeremiah writes of God's judgment as a result of the Israelites' sin and rebellion. Not unlike Jesus' tone in our passage for today, the Book of Lamentations is sorrowful and distressing. But another theme can be found in Lamentations—"the hope found in God's compassion."[3] We see the same compassion in Jesus here in Luke 13:34 as He expresses His deep and tender longing for reconciliation with humanity.

Is Jesus' lament for those who have loved Him or those who have rejected Him?

Can you recall a time when you turned away from Jesus or your faith in God? If so, describe it briefly:

Jesus is expressing sorrow for those who kill God's prophets—those who soon would kill him. Though we may not consider ourselves in that category, we all have denied or rejected Him in one way or another. It is striking and humbling to remember that even when we deny Jesus, He still longs to bring us comfort and protection. There is nothing we can do to nullify His love and compassion for us.

Take a moment to thank Jesus that His love is unending, and that these words of Psalm 103 ring as true for us as they did for rebellious Jerusalem:

> [11]*As high as the heavens are above the earth,*
>   *so great is his love for those who fear him;*
> [12]*as far as the east is from the west,*
>   *so far has he removed our transgressions from us.*
>
> [13]*As a father has compassion on his children,*
>   *so the* LORD *has compassion on those who fear him;*
> [14]*for he knows how we are formed,*
>   *he remembers that we are dust.*
>
> (Psalm 103:11-14)

How does the awareness that we serve a compassionate Savior who remembers the limitations of our humanity affect the way you view Jesus? Does it change the way you communicate with Him? Does it change the language of your prayers?

Based on Jesus' words from today's reading, what do you think kept Him steadfast in His mission to continue on to Jerusalem where the cross awaited?

Jesus concludes this conversation with a quotation from the Hebrew Scriptures. Read Luke 13:35 and fill in the blanks below:

"_____ is he who comes in the

_____ of the _____."

The words Jesus is quoting come from Psalm 118:

> [22]*The stone which the builders rejected*
> *Has become the chief corner stone.*
> [23]*This is the* LORD's *doing;*
> *It is marvelous in our eyes.*
> [24]*This is the day which the* LORD *has made;*
> *Let us rejoice and be glad in it.*
> [25]*O* LORD, *do save, we beseech You;*
> *O* LORD, *we beseech You, do send prosperity!*
> [26]*Blessed is the one who comes in the name of the* LORD;
> *We have blessed you from the house of the Lord.*
>   (Psalm 118:22-26 NASB)

Jesus is the stone that has been rejected. He will become the chief cornerstone of the entire kingdom of God. He will do so because God wills it. This is His heavenly Father's doing; and it will remain marvelous to us because you and I know He was determined to see it through, even when He would face constant opposition and rejection. Obedience to His Father, a desire to bring salvation to the world, and a deep longing to gather God's children as a hen gathers her young would keep Him steadfast. Jesus knows the brokenness of humanity. He feels it in His soul as fully man and fully God. He won't turn back. His compassion for humanity spurs Him forward.

Extra Insight

Jesus' reference to a desolate house in Luke 13:35 is likely a prophecy concerning the coming destruction of the Jewish temple in AD 70.[4]

I Must Keep Going

"Mom, I wish you could be at school with me."

Any mother who has heard these words knows the weight of watching her child grow up. I hear them sometimes from my son as he navigates the tension of adolescence. He enjoys the new freedoms that have come with maturing, but there are times when he longs for the comfort of his childhood. Independence can only be learned on your own. Sometimes letting go will be the hardest task of motherhood. We can't always be there to protect our children. And our hearts break when they come home hurt, disappointed, and a little bruised from the realities of life. But a broken heart only serves to propel us toward shepherding them well. Mothers are determined to love their children.

Just as a mother loves her child, Jesus longs to protect His people. His heart is compassionate toward humanity, and He won't rest until we are gathered under His wing. You and I are called to hold our sisters and brothers with the same compassion. When our hearts are broken for humanity, our commitment to living like Jesus is more steadfast.

This will be what motivates us forward—obedience to God, a desire to see His salvation brought to the world, and a deep longing to comfort broken people. When we see people hurting, struggling, and trying to make sense of disappointment and heartache, we should want to show them Jesus. He knows how to gather them under His wing.

Is Jesus calling you to love the broken today? Do you need a reminder of why it is so important that we remain steadfast in our mission to live like Jesus in every moment? Let's use some of the phraseology from Luke 13:32-33 to commit ourselves to this mission.

Where is Jesus calling you today? Answer this question by filling in the blank below.

I will _____,
and I will reach my goal. I must press on and keep going today and tomorrow and the next day, because I am determined to remain steadfast in my commitment to living like Jesus.

Jesus, break my heart for the people around me who need Your healing. Help me remain steadfast in living like You, showing them Your tender heart for the world. Help me bring hope and lead them to You.

DAY 4: LIVING WITH GRACE

It was my junior year of college. I sat huddled around a small table in a coffee house in Chapel Hill, North Carolina, with Sara and Yvonne, two friends from my campus fellowship group, and our leader, Camper. Once a week, we gathered over a steaming cup of caffeinated goodness to talk about our faith. Camper said it was a discipling group, although I had no idea what that was at the time.

Our goal was not unlike what we are after in this study. We were learning how to live like Jesus. We wanted to become His modern-day disciples. We often read and discussed books, and I'll never forget the first one we opened together. There we sat that day discussing Philip Yancey's *What's So Amazing About Grace*, when I realized the incredible gift it is to have a place at a table where I don't deserve to belong. He writes that "grace means there is nothing I can do to make God love me more, and nothing I can do to make God love me less. It means that I, even I who deserve the opposite, am invited to take my place at the table in God's family."[1]

For a girl who sometimes considered herself an outsider to the church community because I didn't come from the *typical* Christian home, this was a radical idea to me. Jesus has since taught me that the typical Christian home is a myth but His radical grace is an unchanging certainty!

Read Luke 15:11-31, and put a placeholder there for future reference.

The Quick Three
What happened?
Where did it happen?
What characters are mentioned in this reading?

Setting the Scene

Much to the disappointment of the Pharisees and religious teachers, Jesus has returned to his favorite setting as he dines with those outside of society's accepted standards (Luke 15:1-2). He will share three parables concerning lost valuables with them: the lost sheep, the lost coin, and the lost son.

Just as Luke is increasing the storytelling tension as we get closer to Jerusalem, the intensity of these three parables increases as Jesus teaches each one. The shepherd loses one sheep out of a hundred. The woman loses one coin out of ten. But the father in today's reading loses one son out of his only two. The value of the loss is greater with each story.

We have already examined inheritance laws together. You might recall that Deuteronomy 21:17 reveals the details of the law. Since the father had two sons, he would split his estate into three equal parts. One commentator notes that by Jewish law, he would give two parts (a "double-portion") to his oldest son, and the younger son would get the remaining third. It would have been culturally taboo for the younger son to ask for his inheritance while his father was still alive, but he does it anyway.[2]

Even more shocking is that the father agrees. We will see that this parable is a beautiful picture of God's gift of grace.

Lost and Found

Before we dig into the parable of the lost-and-found son, take a minute to think about your understanding of grace.

If you were describing it to a third grader, how would you explain your understanding of biblical *grace*?

Let's begin by examining the three characters in this parable: their actions, their attitudes, and the implications for their moral character.

Read the Scriptures given for each character, and complete the chart to develop a full sense of the decisions each character makes.

Character	What were his actions?	What was his attitude?	What does this tell us about his character?	Which character from Jesus' ministry is most represented by this person?
The Father Luke 15:11-12; Luke 15:20, 22-24, 28, 31-32				(circle one) God The sinners & tax collectors Jesus dines with The self-righteous religious leaders who reject Jesus

Character	What were his actions?	What was his attitude?	What does this tell us about his character?	Which character from Jesus' ministry is most represented by this person?
The Younger Son Luke 15:12-21				(circle one) God The sinners & tax collectors Jesus dines with The self-righteous religious leaders who reject Jesus
The Older Son Luke 15:25-30				(circle one) God The sinners & tax collectors Jesus dines with The self-righteous religious leaders who reject Jesus

After reviewing this parable of grace, pause for a moment to consider a time when God has shown *you* abundant grace. Describe it here, and take a minute to thank Him for it.

Now, let's hone in and consider a few details and insights for each character.

The Father

The father in Jesus' parable is a beautiful example of grace.

Luke 15:20 notes that the father recognized the younger son returning even as he was "a long way off." What does this suggest about the father's heart toward his younger son?

How did the father approach his younger son, and what additional insight does this give us?

We can imagine the father remaining hopeful and routinely watching the horizon for the return of his son and we should not dismiss the fact that the father chose to run as soon as he sees him. One commentator notes that "it was a breach of an elderly Jewish man's dignity to run, though familial love could take priority over dignity after a long absence."[3] This was not a father who was angry. This was a father who was overjoyed to see his son returning home, one who would sacrifice anything to welcome him with open arms.

The Younger Son

The younger son in Jesus' parable is repentant after recognizing his mistakes.

Look closely at the younger son's planned dialogue with his father in Luke 15:18-19 and his actual words in Luke 15:21. What didn't he say?

Noting what follows in Luke 15:22-24, why was the younger son unable to finish his planned request?

Choosing one-word descriptors, how would you characterize the scene the father is commanding?

Oh, the grace of a compassionate father! The son couldn't even make his request to return as hired help because the father was too quick to extend grace. And such abundant grace at that! The scene was extravagant, unrestrained, lavish, costly, joyful, jubilant, and exultant.

The Older Son

The older son is threatened by the grace given to his brother.

Why does the older son refuse to join the party in Luke 15:28?

The older son reacts as if the younger son's actions and the father's response pose a threat to his status in the family. Have you ever seen similar

Extra Insight

The ring given to the younger son by the father likely symbolized a "reinstatement to sonship" into the family.[4]

reactions within the body of Christ? If so, why do you think some feel threatened when someone who has sinned is treated with grace?

What about you? Where do you see yourself in this story? Which response do you most identify with today?

__ Wandering away from God and acting out in rebellion

__ Intentionally pursuing and enthusiastically welcoming those who have made mistakes

__ Rejecting those who aren't making the "right" choices

We will likely identify with all three characters at varying points in our life. Sometimes we'll get it right, and other times we'll fail miserably. All the time, we should aim to extend the same grace and forgiveness to ourselves that we need to extend to others.

In his New Testament commentary *Be Courageous: Take Heart from Christ's Example*, pastor and theologian Warren Wiersbe writes,

> In my years of preaching and pastoral ministry, I have met elder brothers (and sisters!) who have preferred nursing their anger to enjoying the fellowship of God and God's people. Because they will not forgive, they have alienated themselves from the church and even from their family; they are sure that everyone else is wrong and they alone are right. They can talk loudly about the sins of others, but they are blind to their own sins.
>
> "I never forgive!" General Oglethorpe said to John Wesley, to which Wesley replied, "Then, sir, I hope you never sin."[5]

Read the verses below, drawing from them to make a list of defining attributes for grace.

Grace is . . .

John 1:14

Romans 5:6-10

Romans 11:5-6

Ephesians 2:8

Ephesians 4:7

2 Thessalonians 2:16

Open Arms

I walked through a season recently when I needed an abundant supply of energy, much more than I knew myself to be capable of. A family member was going through a crisis, and she needed welcoming arms and extra attention to see her through it. I was ill-equipped to meet her needs and made several mistakes along the way, trying to help her. I thought the answer was that I simply needed more energy, so that's what I asked God for. Lord, *give me a double-portion of Your energy to sustain me through this crisis.*

What He gave me instead was a double-portion of grace.

Like the young son, we sometimes think we know the solutions to our problems. We may even boldly request them of the Lord. But He knows what we need most and is ready and willing to give it to us.

We will *always* be a people who need grace. The moment we forget that is the moment we stop being effective witnesses for the kingdom of God. His loving determination to rescue people everywhere motivates us to welcome the repentant heart with open arms.

God is still looking for those who are a long way off. He is still waiting expectantly for the repentant to return. He is preparing the best robe, fashioning the finest ring, and assembling the most lavish feast. He's simply waiting for us to invite them to the table.

Is there someone you have deemed "too far gone" to be rescued? Is there someone you think is impossible to reach for God? If so, write a prayer for this person now, determining to welcome him or her with open arms.

God's loving determination to rescue people everywhere motivates us to welcome the repentant heart with open arms.

They might not come home today. But when they do, let's be ready to flood them with the same grace we have received from our heavenly Father. Nothing that they have done can negate the Father's love. It shouldn't undo our love either.

Close today by writing one more prayer, asking Jesus to move in your heart as you consider His tremendous gift of grace for all people:

Jesus, thank You for Your unending grace over my life. Forgive me for

_____.

Make me aware of the actions of others that I need to forgive. Help me to forgive others for these actions that have wounded me:

_____

_____.

Make me aware of those who need to see grace. May I show grace by

_____

_____ .

Help me to lavish them with abundant grace. Give me opportunities to love them well and invite them to Your table. Amen.

DAY 5: REDEFINING HUMILITY

I didn't realize the depth of my need for Jesus until I had to constantly rely on Him to see me through the day, sixty minutes at a time. Sixty minutes was about as long as I could last before another wave of panic would hit. As the clock approached the top of each hour, my heart would begin to pound, my ears would ring, and my chest would be so tight I could barely catch my breath. Living with a condition that promises major medical events proved too much for my notions of self-reliance. Only Jesus could get me through to the next moment.

So, I set my phone with an hourly alarm. When it rang, I stopped what I was doing to open my Bible and pray, pleading for Jesus to calm my anxious mind. And that's how I got through the darkest three months of my life—sixty minutes at a time, relying on the only true source of peace: Jesus Christ.

Before God called me into full-time ministry, I made a living as a fitness instructor, teaching other people how to be healthy and manage daily stress. I had a lot of tangible tricks up my sleeve to help battle my anxiety, but none of them were as powerful as falling before the throne of Jesus to rely on Him completely for my next breath.

I needed Him then. I need Him now.

Read Luke 18:9-17, and put a placeholder there for future reference.

The Quick Three
What happened?
Where did it happen?
What characters are mentioned in this reading?

Setting the Scene

Yesterday's lesson left us with the image of God's welcoming arms. Today will be no different. Jesus welcomes all people, and He is particularly accepting of the "least of these" (Matthew 15:40). But what, exactly, does He welcome them into?

This isn't the first time we have seen Jesus mention the kingdom of God, and it won't be the last. We could dedicate an entire study to the exploration of that term; even the most brilliant biblical scholars struggle to thoroughly define it. But let's unpack it just a bit before we continue, because we'll need to have a basic understanding of God's kingdom to fully grasp Jesus' teaching for today.

The Lord has established his throne in heaven, and his kingdom rules over all.
(Psalm 103:19)

Scripture tells us that the kingdom of God is both spiritual and physical. It involves the submission of our hearts to the will of God and the acknowledgment that He is in control of all that is seen and unseen. We saw Jesus introduce the kingdom of God in His manifesto when we studied Luke 4 together and Psalm 103:19 reinforces the image of God's royal reign. Let's take a closer look at what the Gospel of Luke teaches about the kingdom of God.

The Gospel of Luke tells us that the kingdom of God:

- is good news (Luke 4:43),
- requires steadfast determination (Luke 9:62),
- is open to all (Luke 13:29),
- is a present reality (Luke 17:21),
- has not been brought to full completion yet (Luke 21:31),
- demands sacrifice (Luke 17:33) and a repentant heart (Luke 24:47).

You will find many other truths about the kingdom of God in the Gospel of Luke, but in today's reading, Jesus presents us with two contrasting characters—one who is fit for the kingdom of God, and one who is not. There is another requirement for citizenship in God's kingdom not mentioned above. Not surprisingly, this requirement is rarely found within humanity but is attainable to those who want to live like Jesus: humility.

An Ideal Citizen

Humility is a characteristic that requires total dependence on God.

On a scale of 1-10, with 1 being the least and 10 being the most, how would you rate your dependence on God today?

1   2   3   4   5   6   7   8   9   10

Jesus is teaching once again by employing a parable. In Luke 18:10, who are the two characters in His story?

These two characters represent two extremes of society. As a religious leader, the Pharisee was among the most esteemed and respected, while the tax collector would have been one of the most despised people in Jewish society.[1] It's interesting to note that the prayer of the Pharisee in the parable is not that different from an *actual* prayer of a first-century rabbi found in *The Life and Times of Jesus the Messiah* by Alfred Edersheim:

> I thank Thee, O Lord my God, that Thou hast put my part with those who sit in the Academy, and not with those who sit at the corners [money-changers and traders]. For, I rise early and they rise early: I rise early to the words of the Law, and they to vain things. I labour and they labour: I labour and receive a reward, they labour and receive no reward. I run and they run: I run to the life of the world to come, and they to the pit of destruction.[2]

Compare Luke 18:11-12 to the prayer above. What similarities do you notice between these two prayers?

How would you describe each prayer?

The prayer of the Pharisee:

The prayer of the first-century rabbi:

On a scale of 1-10, with 1 being the least and 10 being the most, how would you rate the Pharisee's dependence on God?

1   2   3   4   5   6   7   8   9   10

Explain your rating below:

Compare the actions of the tax collector in Luke 18:13 with the words of the prophet in Isaiah 6:5 (in the margin). What similarities do you notice between the two?

"Woe to me!" I cried. "I am ruined! For I am a man of unclean lips, and I live among a people of unclean lips, and my eyes have seen the King, the LORD Almighty." (Isaiah 6:5)

Extra Insight

"Beating one's breast was a sign of great mourning or grief, in this case [with the tax collector], in repentance for sin (which in Jewish custom was expressed by mourning)."[3]

On a scale of 1-10, with 1 being the least and 10 being the most, how would you rate the tax collector's dependence on God?

1   2   3   4   5   6   7   8   9   10

Explain your rating below:

In Luke 18:14, Jesus tells us that only a certain type of person will be exalted. What quality will he or she possess?

Of the two characters Jesus presented in this parable, which one demonstrates humility, and how?

In the Book of Philippians, the Apostle Paul contends that to live like Christ, we must first adopt His humble attitude.

Read the following passage and underline any actions that demonstrate humility.

[5]Have this attitude in yourselves which was also in Christ Jesus, [6]who, although He existed in the form of God, did not regard equality with God a thing to be grasped, [7]but emptied Himself, taking the form of a bond-servant, and being made in the likeness of men. [8]Being found in appearance as a man, He humbled Himself by becoming obedient to the point of death, even death on a cross. [9]For this reason also, God highly exalted Him, and bestowed on Him the name which is above every name, [10]so that at the name of Jesus EVERY KNEE WILL BOW, of those who are in heaven and on earth and under the earth, [11]and that every tongue will confess that Jesus Christ is Lord, to the glory of God the Father.

(Philippians 2:5-11 NASB)

Just in case Jesus' parable—not to mention His own living example—was not enough, Luke transitions to a scene that gives us the perfect picture of humility: Jesus surrounded by children. His disciples were not too happy about it and, in fact, had rebuked them likely because they were trying to protect Jesus from a long line of parents seeking a blessing for their little ones.[4] But Jesus welcomed them with open arms. The remarkable thing about this scene is that in Jewish society, children held no special status and often were seen as the "least valuable" since they contributed little to the overall good.[5]

Read Luke 18:16-17. What does Jesus say about the kingdom of God in these verses?

Extra Insight

For a deeper discussion on the kingdom of God, see Luke 17:20-37.

It would not have gone unnoticed to Jesus' observers that He willingly accepted a long line of those who were deemed as unworthy of His time. In addition to their innocent willingness to believe, children remain totally dependent on their parents for all their physical, emotional, and spiritual needs. They were and are the least, yet Jesus hails them as ideal citizens in the kingdom of God. If we want to join them as residents of God's kingdom, we will have to admit that we, too, must rely on God for our every need.

When considering things such as big decisions, finances, conflict resolution, and the fulfillment of your desires, how easy or difficult is it for you to depend on God? Explain your response.

Opening Our Eyes

Something peculiar happened in the three months that I set my hourly alarm to pray as I battled with anxiety. I learned that total reliance on God brought inexpressible wonder. Every refocus on God's power brought reverence for the gifts that would unfold in the next hour. There is a reason why secure children are filled with uncontainable joy. Because they are unhindered by the burden of self-reliance, they have the mental and emotional margin to simply sit in the wondrous truth that someone else is in control. Likewise, when we rely fully on God, we can rest in the humble truth that He is King.

Today, humility is often referred to with a negative perception. The concept of lowering oneself is the antithesis of all that is touted in our culture. But the gift of humility is that it allows us to welcome the "least of these" just as Jesus did. Humbly admitting our total dependence on God opens our eyes to the most vulnerable among us.

This will be a three-step process.

1. *Admit your needs to God.* The first step toward humility is to admit that we need God in every aspect of our lives. What do you need Jesus' help with today? You might identify it by asking yourself these questions:

- What have I been trying to accomplish in my own strength?
- Is my greatest source of inspiration currently not found in God's presence or Word? What am I looking to instead of God?

Humbly admitting our total dependence on God opens our eyes to the most vulnerable among us.

- Are my thoughts and prayers overly self-focused? What do I spend most of my time thinking and praying about?
- What area of my life is bringing tension?

2. *Surrender these things to Jesus now.* Take a moment to pray about anything that has come to mind as we have studied today. Surrender it to Jesus, acknowledging that you will rely on His strength alone to see you through.

3. *Open your eyes to those around you.* When we recognize our own need for Jesus, it is easy to see the same needs in others. Ask Jesus to reveal those in your life who are the most vulnerable, and then ask Him to show you tangible ways you can point them to His saving love and grace.

Let's close by meditating on Isaiah 46:4, thanking God for sustaining us in every way:

> *Even to your old age and gray hairs*
> *I am he, I am he who will sustain you.*
> *I have made you and I will carry you;*
> *I will sustain you and I will rescue you.*
> (Isaiah 46:4)

As we end this week and head into our final week of study, I want you to know how proud I am of you for determining to keep going on our journey to living like Jesus!

Luke 19:1-10

Sometimes when we don't know what we _____, we climb a tree because it's easier to look from afar than welcome the truth.

Jesus gives the highest place of _____ to the least expected recipient.

Jesus came to seek and save, not _____ and _____.

Week 6

The Victor

Determined to Live with Courage

(Luke 19; 20; 22–24)

> **The one who says he remains in him should walk just as he walked.**
> **(1 John 2:6 CSB)**

When my son was a toddler, he would walk the beach with us by stepping his tiny feet into my husband's footprints. Even when my husband's long legs would take him far ahead of us, my son knew the way because he simply followed his father's footsteps. He never questioned the path before him because he trusted the person who had walked it first.

During the past five weeks, we have traced the footprints of Jesus. In our final week of study together, we'll follow those footprints to the cross.

Every one of them was planted with purpose. Not one footprint was wasted. Every step forward led Jesus to His ultimate goal of proclaiming good news for the entire world. Though we read the passage below early in our study, I offer it now as a reminder of what Jesus was determined to accomplish.

> [18]*"The Spirit of the Lord is upon me,*
> *because he has anointed me*
> *to proclaim good news to the poor.*
> *He has sent me to proclaim liberty to the captives*
> *and recovering of sight to the blind,*
> *to set at liberty those who are oppressed,*
> [19]*to proclaim the year of the Lord's favor."*
> (Luke 4:18-19 ESV)

Sister, the year of the Lord's favor is here. It has been here since Jesus walked the streets of Bethlehem, Capernaum, the shores of Galilee, and the roads through Samaria. It rejoices triumphant in the heart of Jerusalem. And it reigns over you today. Let it crown you with peace and joy, but let it also crown you with courage.

You and I both know that there is hardship ahead—for Jesus, and perhaps for you too. Whatever you bring with you into this final week of study, there is no need to fear. Jesus has already been there and achieved victory over it. He does not call us into places where His feet have not already marched. Our job is simply to fit our footsteps into His.

While there may be sorrow ahead, there is sweet victory to come. We can cling to this truth because we serve the one, true King of the world. There is nothing He won't fight in order to see you safely home, and there is nothing He cannot defeat. Would you allow Him to light the way for your next footstep today? Even if the path is foreign to you, Jesus has walked it. He knows the way and is determined to lead you in it. All you have to do is follow the King.

DAY 1: DEFIANCE AND COURAGE

> And I will put enmity
> Between you and the woman,
> And between your seed and her seed;
> He shall bruise you on the head,
> And you shall bruise him on the heel.
> (Genesis 3:15 NASB)

What began with these ominous words from the Creator of the universe to the enemy of our souls would one day reach its climax in what we are studying together this week—the last week of our Savior's earthly ministry. Even in the first few pages of the Bible, the path for Jesus had been set. Throughout the Old Testament we find repeated prophecies of the One who was determined to redeem mankind, although He wouldn't face that task until the exact moment that God had ordained it.

The timer had been set. The clock was ticking. A divine appointment was scheduled for Jesus in Jerusalem, one that had been foretold from the very beginning. Flip your way from Genesis through the Bible and you'll read not only of the unfathomable love of God for His creation but also of His determination to save it through His Son, the coming Messiah. Jesus has *always* been part of the story.

We see this same determination in Jesus, and today we will find Him to be defiantly courageous. "Blessed is the king who comes in the name of the Lord!" (Luke 19:38).

Read Luke 19:28-44, and put a placeholder there for future reference.

The Quick Three
What happened?
Where did it happen?
What characters are mentioned in this reading?

Setting the Scene

Much happens during Jesus' final week on earth. One source outlines the events this way:

Sunday – Triumphal entry into Jerusalem
Monday – Cleansing the temple
Tuesday – Controversies with the Jewish leaders
Wednesday – Apparently a day of rest
Thursday – Preparation for Passover
Friday – Trial and crucifixion
Saturday – Jesus rests in the tomb
Sunday – Jesus raised from the dead[1]

Tensions were mounting in Jerusalem. John 9:22 tells us that Jewish leaders were openly punishing anyone who professed Jesus as Messiah. His return to Jerusalem had to be executed carefully, but it was not without royal jubilee. The King had come to take His throne.

As we learned in Week 1, Jewish families traveled to Jerusalem every year to celebrate the Passover. In fact, it was during the season of the Passover festival that twelve-year-old Jesus insisted with determination that He had to be about His Father's business—his first recorded words (Luke 2:49). Here in Luke 19 it is Passover season again as He returns to Jerusalem once more, and we will see His characteristic determination in full force.

Determination Is a Godly Trait

None of the details in our reading for today were insignificant. Thousands of years of prophecy culminated in this exact moment in time. Let's consider some of the details together—details that will highlight how God is always working for our good and show us that determination in the face of difficulty is a godly trait.

Time of the Passover (Luke 19:28)

Our reading begins in Luke 19:28, where we learn that Jesus is "going up to Jerusalem," and we know from the surrounding chapters that the purpose was to celebrate the Passover festival. Though His followers did not understand the suffering that lay ahead—even though He had told them in Luke 9:21-22—Jesus knew what He soon would be facing.

Read Matthew 26:3-5. What do these verses tell us about the religious leaders' original intended timing for Jesus' arrest?

The religious leaders did not want to arrest Jesus during the crowded Passover season because they feared a riot from His supporters. But as we will see, they will change their plan. Jesus would serve as the Passover Lamb, the final sacrifice for the sins of the world (1 Corinthians 5:7).

The Donkey (Luke 19:30)

Jesus' first order of business upon entering the city was to procure a donkey for His triumphant entry.

What do 1 Kings 1:32-34, 44 tell us about one use for donkeys or mules?

It was not an accident that Jesus rode into Jerusalem on a donkey. First, it fulfilled Zechariah's prophecy, which would ring in the ears of those wise enough to remember it:

Rejoice greatly, Daughter Zion!
   Shout, Daughter Jerusalem!
See, your king comes to you,
   righteous and victorious,
lowly and riding on a donkey,
   on a colt, the foal of a donkey.
                (*Zechariah 9:9*)

And second, donkeys often had been used by kings in the history of the Israelites.[2] No one watching the scene unfold would miss the meaningful irony of the Messiah riding into a city He had walked into many times before.

The Cloaks (Luke 19:35-36)

Jesus' supporters welcomed Him by spreading their cloaks along the ground as He entered the city.

What does 2 Kings 9:13 tell us about the practice of spreading cloaks on the ground?

The crowds of Jesus' followers pouring into Jerusalem for the season of the Passover festival wanted to honor Him. Some recognized Him as a hoped-for earthly king, while others recognized him as Messiah, the King of kings. Either way, the details of His triumphant return were divinely orchestrated. Just as we see God's hand in these details, so we can also see God's hand in the details of our own lives.

Have you ever felt that the details of your life are insignificant to God? If so, explain why.

Consider the three details we have mentioned above, in addition to evidence found throughout all of Scripture. Some of my favorite stories in the Bible show us how God was always working in the details for the good of those who loved Him. The infant Moses being rescued from Pharaoh (Exodus 2), Rahab's involvement in the Israelites' defeat of Jericho (Joshua 2; 6), or Ruth playing a part in the ancestral line of Jesus (Ruth 4)—each of these stories is a reminder that God is always up to something. He's working in the details even when you can't see the whole picture.

When we're facing the storm, heading into the impossible, God is always working for our good. Just as He allowed Moses' own mother to nurse him after she placed him in the river, thinking she would never see him again; just as He stirred Rahab's heart to open her door to the Israelite spies; just as He provided a job opening for widowed Ruth in the field of the man who would eventually marry her; and just as He carefully orchestrated His Son's entry into Jerusalem, God is always working in the details of our lives. Let's be determined to find Him there—as determined as Jesus was when he entered Jerusalem.

Read Luke 19:41. What is Jesus' response as He approaches Jerusalem?

We have seen Jesus' compassion for Jerusalem previously in Luke 13. Why do you think He weeps now?

Even as He approaches His arduous destiny, Jesus is weeping for the people He loves. And we might even speculate that He is weeping more so for the ones who refuse to love Him.

Let's take a moment to put ourselves in different shoes. First, imagine that you are a Jerusalem citizen and you are *not* a supporter of Jesus. You've heard the outlandish claims of His encounters, but you're not a fan of change and you can't figure this Jesus guy out. You definitely aren't on the front row throwing your cloak down at the feet of His donkey, but you watch from a distance as this visitor from the north enters your hometown.

As this citizen, what would you be thinking right now?

Now, let's switch "sides." Imagine that you are the mother of the beloved son that Jesus brought back to life—or the healed woman who still remembers the sting of twelve years with a bleeding disorder but now knows joy in Jesus. Or perhaps your brother told you how Jesus rescued him from a legion of demons; you live in freedom now too because he told you that the Messiah had finally come. Whoever you are, you've made the journey to Jerusalem with your fellow pilgrims and you follow Jesus into the city, proud and jubilant that your Savior is taking His rightful place on the throne of God's kingdom. You're not aware of the arrest and crucifixion to come, but still you sense in Jesus' heartache as He weeps that something awful is on the way.

As one of these followers, what might you be thinking right now?

Finally, let's consider what Jesus might be thinking. We have some clues in what we've already read in Luke. We'll remember that Jesus knows what awaits Him in just five days. He has known it all along. Yet when He sees the city gates from a distance, not once do His footsteps falter. He knows that the authorities will try to arrest Him quietly. Instead, He forces their hand by riding into a humble but divinely royal celebration. They would have no choice but to respond with legal retribution. R. T. France writes that because of all of the implications of His return to Jerusalem, "Jesus' triumphal entry was a carefully planned act of 'glorious defiance and superlative courage.'"[4]

Make no mistake, sister. Jesus entered the city of Jerusalem as humility-made-manifest, but He did so with His face set like flint. If we have a determined bone in our body today, it's because we inherited it from our heavenly Father just as Jesus did. And when set against a holy backdrop, a holy purpose, determination is a godly trait.

Finding the Strength Within

There is a reason you and I are called to the impossible. It's not because life is hard. It's not because life is unfair. We are called to the impossible because we share spiritual DNA with the One who makes all things possible. Although the situation before Jesus might have appeared to be hopeless, Jesus obediently served the God of hope.

Our mission is the same today. As determined living takes us into situations that seem hopeless, we can find courage in a God who does the impossible.

Like Jesus, we may be weary from years of grueling ministry work, but we can move forward anyway. Tears might be falling from our eyes in sorrow for those we love, but we can move forward anyway. People might question our motives or threaten to stop us, but we can move forward anyway. The road ahead might

As determined living takes us unto situations that seem hopeless, we can find courage in a God who does the impossible.

be excruciating and challenging—it might even demand our very lives—but we can move forward anyway. Why? Because we are born again into a divine family that refuses to give up, and the power of Christ is our inheritance.

> Read the following passages and note what each one teaches us about the indwelling power of Christ.
>
> 2 Corinthians 13:4-6
>
> Galatians 2:20
>
> Ephesians 3:16-18
>
> Colossians 1:27

You, my beloved sister, are not called to the impossible because we live in a broken world. You are called to the impossible because the One who lives inside of you can heal it.

Close today by thanking Jesus for riding into the city of Jerusalem, determined to love us, determined to love the world.

Jesus, give me a defiant heart and courage for the journey ahead. I know You alone are capable of making me determined.

DAY 2: GRACE UNDER PRESSURE

> There's trouble ahead when you live only for the approval of others, saying what flatters them, doing what indulges them. Popularity contests are not truth contests—look how many scoundrel preachers were approved by your ancestors! Your task is to be true, not popular.
> (Luke 6:26 MSG)

I wish these words were not accurate. We've seen them before in Week 2 of our study, but the paraphrased *Message* translation above renders them incredibly relatable for our culture today. Popularity rules if you are willing to sacrifice authenticity for applause.

I have a handful of dear friends I refer to as my truth tellers. They won't hide behind a lie to make me feel better about myself, nor will they tell me only what I want to hear. They lay down the truth, always, and I am thankful for their candid commentary on my life. It has saved my skin more times than I'd like to admit.

But truth tellers aren't always welcomed. If you've ever been opposed by a loved one in a conversation where your advice was biblically sound you know this to be a fact. Not surprisingly, people are hesitant to hear news that threatens their way of life.

Jesus knew that His task was to speak truth. He also knew that this would not make Him popular, at least not among those who were challenged by His truth. But it is possible to speak the truth in love, delivering grace while simultaneously standing for God's Word.

Today Jesus will show us how.

Read Luke 20:1-19, and put a placeholder there for future reference.

The Quick Three
What happened?
Where did it happen?
What characters are mentioned in this reading?

Setting the Scene

We began our study in the Temple courts of Jerusalem, and it is here that we return today. After clearing the Temple of those who had turned it into a marketplace, Jesus settles in to restore it to its original purpose: a place to learn, pray, and worship. The conflict doesn't end with the clearing of the Temple. It is only about to escalate.

Jesus is teaching from the court of the Gentiles, the outer area of Herod's temple that is open to the public.[1] Three groups of challengers have gathered to question Jesus as He is teaching: the chief priests, scribes, and elders. You may remember that these three groups together comprised the Sanhedrin, the governing authority that soon will condemn Jesus to death.[2] We will see that Jesus handles their questions with truth and grace.

The Divine Truth Teller

Before we see how Jesus handled his opposers, let's pause to consider how we tend to respond when facing conflict.

How do you handle conflict with others? Circle the response that is most appropriate:

I avoid it at all costs.

I'll do it if I have to, but I don't enjoy it.

If it's for the right reasons, I won't hesitate to confront someone.

I was on the debate team in high school. Bring it on.

What do you find most challenging about facing conflict?

In Luke 20, the chief priests, teachers of the law, and elders gather before Jesus to question one thing.

What is the root of their opposition with Jesus in Luke 20:2?

Jesus' challengers are in charge of all that happens in the Temple. They have not given Jesus authority to teach in the Temple, and neither have the Romans.[3]

What is the elders' predicament in Luke 20:5-6?

In light of Jesus' words in Luke 6:26 (see the beginning of today's lesson), what could He accuse them of?

What does this passage teach us about Jesus' identity and authority?

Why do you think the religious leaders challenge it?

Warren Wiersbe says this of Jesus' encounter with the Israelite elders:

They wanted to push our Lord into a dilemma so that no matter how He answered, He would be in trouble. If He said that He had no authority, then He was in trouble with the Jews for invading their temple and acting like a prophet. If He said that His authority came from God, then He would be in trouble with the Romans, who were always alert to would-be messiahs, especially during Passover season.[4]

Jesus responded with grace under pressure—and a good dose of wisdom to go with that. His authority may have been challenged, but His brilliance was displayed.

Read the bullets below, noting Jesus' particular response strategy in each situation:

- Jesus is challenged by the Sanhedrin: *"Who gave you this authority?"* *(Luke 20:2)*
  Luke 20:3 – Jesus responds by _____.

- They think they will trick Him by feigning ignorance: *"We don't know where it was from." (Luke 20:7)*
  Luke 20:8 – Jesus responds by _____.

- The people are shocked that what Jesus said might be true: *"May it never be!" (Luke 20:16 NASB)*
  Luke 20:17-18 – Jesus responds by _____.

Review the parable Jesus teaches in Luke 20:9-16. Try to summarize its lesson in one sentence:

If this parable seems like a harsh lesson to you, you're not alone. I find this one hard to read as well. But keep in mind that Jesus stood in the face of great opposition as He told this parable. He used this as an opportunity to deliver a straightforward illustration about what was unfolding before Him—packaged in a story that they would understand well.

The vineyard metaphor would have resonated deeply with His challengers.

Read Isaiah 5:1-7. What does the vineyard represent in this passage?

In Jesus' parable, each character symbolizes someone or something within God's greater story of bringing salvation for the world. Who or what do you think each character symbolizes?

The vineyard planter:

The tenant farmers:

The servants sent by the vineyard planter:

The vineyard planter's son:

The others who inherit the vineyard:

Although impossible to fathom at the time, Jesus' parable implied that the religious leaders would face destruction and separation from God while the kingdom of God would be given to those who believed and followed Him.[5] Even though Jesus knows with certainty how they will respond, there is a veiled exhortation to the religious leaders within the parable: *You can repent. God is merciful. Trust in me as the foundation to your faith, and you will be spared the destruction that is foretold.*

What was the response from the Sanhedrin in Luke 20:19?

Graceful Confrontation

Today's passage is intricately woven with contextual innuendos and cultural implications. But Jesus' clever responses and uncompromising dedication to speaking the truth are what shine through. Rather than pose a direct accusation, Jesus responds by telling a story—one that would communicate truth to his listeners who had questioned His authority. Luke shares the account not only to advance the tension in the story toward the coming crucifixion but also to highlight our Savior's unquestionable authority and abiding determination in the face of opposition.

You and I will have to engage in disagreements with those we love and those we struggle to love. In a world filled with different opinions, priorities, and influences, this is a given. We will face rejection and opposition as we seek to live like Jesus. Sometimes the opposition we face will be solely *because* we are seeking to live like Jesus. But we can always choose to speak the truth in love. When we cling to Jesus, we can boldly confront difficult situations with wisdom and grace. As the Apostle Paul writes,

> [14] *Then we will no longer be infants, tossed back and forth by the waves, and blown here and there by every wind of teaching and by the cunning and craftiness of people in their deceitful scheming.* [15] *Instead, speaking the truth in love, we will grow to become in every respect the mature body of him who is the head, that is, Christ.* [16] *From him the whole body, joined and held together by every supporting ligament, grows and builds itself up in love, as each part does its work.*
>
> (Ephesians 4:14-16)

As we close today, I'd like to highlight three observations we can take from Jesus' example:

1. **Jesus was not afraid of conflict**. He didn't promote it, but He didn't shy away from it either. If conflict has arrived at our front door, we don't need to fear it.

When we cling to Jesus, we can boldly confront difficult situations with wisdom and grace.

2. **Jesus relied on biblical wisdom to hold His position.** He didn't justify His presence at the Temple by offering defensive excuses. He went straight to the heart of the matter by focusing on His divine authority, using wisdom imparted from a God-appointed prophet as an example.

3. **Jesus used the presence of conflict to point others to the character of God.** Always the teacher, He knew that the knowledge of God had the power to change someone's life. He aimed to glorify God in every word He spoke.

Although Jesus' parable doesn't leave much room for grace toward the tenant farmers, this is only because He knows exactly what the religious leaders are about to do: arrest Him, which is the equivalent of rejecting His truth. We have seen the entire ministry of Jesus uphold the reality that God's grace reigns supreme. So we should not interpret this parable as meaning that there are exceptions to God's grace. Redemption is *always* available to the repentant heart. Rather, this parable reminds us that there are consequences for those who continue to reject God's truth with hard hearts, which should motivate us to seek and uphold truth with grace and compassion for our neighbors. May we also remember the wisdom of Proverbs 15:1, that "a gentle answer turns away wrath, / but a harsh word stirs up anger." With gentleness as our guide, we can face opposition with graceful determination.

Is there a situation you are dealing with now that is bringing conflict into your life? If so, how might you face it with graceful determination?

Close today by spending some time in prayer over any situation that is causing conflict for you or those you love. Ask Jesus to cover it with His grace as He gives you the wisdom to know when to step forward as a truth teller and the courage to speak the truth in love.

DAY 3: CHANGED FOR GOOD

> [8]Now the Lord God had planted a garden in the east, in Eden; and there he put the man he had formed. [9]The Lord God made all kinds of trees grow out of the ground—trees that were pleasing to the eye and good for food. In the middle of the garden were the tree of life and the tree of the knowledge of good and evil.
> (Genesis 2:8-9)

My favorite walking spot is a small garden tucked on the outskirts of the capital city near my home. It is quiet and peaceful, and it is rare to find it heavily populated—so much so that I sometimes imagine there is a secret entrance code that only a handful of us know, giving access to a private oasis reserved for the few who appreciate its gifts.

It is carefully maintained by the city and is the most beautifully landscaped public garden I've ever been to; and as a nature lover, I've seen my fair share of lovely gardens. I don't come there to exercise; I slowly walk the cemented paths to pray. It is a meditative space, inviting intimacy with the Creator of all that flourishes around me as I walk. Time stills when I am there; and if my daily obligations allow for lingering, I'll always indulge with an extra loop around the garden.

While I know it doesn't compare to the paradise that Adam and Eve once knew, I imagine that this is what the garden of Eden felt like. The union of the presence of both God and people, it was a heavenly utopia that humanity has craved for all these years since the consequences of sin revoked access to its treasures.

What began in a garden is about to end in a garden.

Only this time the consequences will be reversed. The determined One will absorb the full weight of our sin so that we might walk, once more, in paradise.

Read Luke 22:39-53, and put a placeholder there for future reference.

The Quick Three
What happened?
Where did it happen?
What characters are mentioned in this reading?

Setting the Scene

Since Jesus' confrontation with the Sanhedrin, He now will be spied on and plotted against as He continues to give final teachings to His disciples and those listening in the Temple. Persuaded by Satan, Judas agrees to betray Jesus (Luke 22:3-6), yet Jesus welcomes him to the Last Supper still. He knows what must occur.

Located off the eastern wall of the Temple and nestled in the Mount of Olives, the garden of Gethsemane was a fifteen-minute walk from the location of the upper room where Jesus and the disciples had their last supper together.[1]

Luke tells us that Jesus traveled there "as was His custom" (Luke 22:39 NASB). It was a walk that He had taken often. He knew the garden well and had sought solace there before, which is why Judas knew exactly where to lead the arresting army to find Him (John 18:1-2).

Jesus had been followed by crowds His entire ministry. But the crowd that approached Him in the garden of Gethsemane would be different. They came with swords and clubs. Were they worried Jesus' followers would revolt? That Jesus might perform a miracle? Or perhaps their weapons were merely an outward display of the dread that might have seized their hearts.

Acts of the dark are never done without fear. But somehow, this one would lead to ultimate good for all.

Rise, Anyway

We've noted already Jesus' habit for solitude and prayer. Now, more than ever, He would need both to carry Him through what is to come.

What did Jesus ask His disciples to do in Luke 22:40?

Leaving His disciples to pray, Jesus finds a quiet spot and prays by Himself.

Write Jesus' prayer found in Luke 22:42 here word for word:

Read the following passages and note how each might relate to Jesus' prayer in the garden:

Psalm 75:8

Isaiah 51:17-23

Scholars note that "Jesus elsewhere refers to the cross as his cup (Mark 14:23-24, 36), which may allude to the cup of judgment that appears often in the Old Testament."[3] (See Psalm 60:3; Isaiah 51:17-23; and Jeremiah 25:15-29 as examples.) It might also be an image fresh on His mind as He has just offered a cup of wine to His disciples in the Last Supper.

What does the cup in Luke 22:20 represent?

Why does the angel appear in Luke 22:43?

Even though He was fully divine, Jesus struggled with His fate because he was also fully human. This task would require heavenly assistance from God Himself to complete. God knows what it means to face extreme anxiety, but He always equips us, His children, with what we need to stay the course.

When we are in a similar mindset, one of the greatest lies we sometimes tell ourselves is that we are alone in our suffering. And it's exactly that: a lie. Be bold enough to look a stranger in the eye today with kindness. When you do, you just may see that you carry similar burdens. Their burdens might not have the same labels as yours, but you live in the same broken world and carry the same effects of that brokenness: hurt. My hurt is your hurt is their hurt.

Can you recall a time when you felt like you were facing difficulty alone?
If so, describe it briefly below:

We don't just share our hurt with humanity. The word used in Luke 22:44 to describe Jesus' emotions as He prepared to face the cross is *anguish* or *agony*. The Greek transliteration used here for anguish is *agónia*, which means "great fear, terror, of death; anxiety, agony."[4]

Jesus understands our anxiety and sorrow over the most difficult of tasks. He knows what it's like to feel the heart pounding between uneven and shallow breaths. He even knows what it feels like to sweat blood. Not once does He hear your prayer for relief and respond with trite and pithy instructions to "shake it off" or "get over it." When you think that no one around you understands, remember that your Savior does because He has lived it in the flesh. The writer of Hebrews tells us,

> [7]*During the days of Jesus' life on earth, he offered up prayers and petitions with* **fervent cries and tears** *to the one who could save him from death, and he was heard because of his reverent submission.* [8]*Son though he was, he learned obedience from what he suffered* [9]*and, once made perfect, he became the source of eternal salvation for all who obey him* [10]*and was designated by God to be high priest in the order of Melchizedek.*
>
> (5:7-10, *emphasis added*)

The fervent cries and tears of Jesus were lifted up to heaven. And then after praying, He stood up. The strength and determination alone it would have taken Him to rise in the garden humbles me to the core.

Extra Insight

Luke's use of the word *like* in Luke 22:44 could imply that Jesus' sweat fell to the ground *like* drops of blood or it could suggest actual *hematidrosis*, a rare condition that causes tiny blood vessel ruptures in the sweat glands due to tremendous emotional stress.[5]

Read Luke 22:45-53, and list the sequence of Jesus' actions after praying:

Does Jesus fight His accusers or willingly go with them?

We may not understand God's will for us. We might not even *want* God's will for us. But we serve a King who was determined to obey His Father's will *anyway*, and we can do the same.

How would you complete the following? Circle the underlined option that fits best:

The desires of my heart <u>often</u> / <u>sometimes</u> / <u>hardly ever</u> match God's will for my life.

Why?

No matter what we are facing today, we can determine to...

Live anyway.
Testify anyway.
Serve anyway.
Rise in the morning anyway.
Obey anyway.
Do it anyway.

To choose life anyway in the face of tremendous opposition is the ultimate display of living like Jesus.

What is your "anyway" today? Fill in the blank below.

I will _____ anyway.

Trading Our Desires for Divine Will

Take delight in the LORD, and he will give you the desires of your heart.

(Psalm 37:4)

Scripture promises that if we delight ourselves in the Lord, He will give us the desires of our hearts (Psalm 37:4). But this doesn't mean that our desires will always match the will of God. It implies that the more we spend time in communion with God, the more He will shape our desires to match His will. Until our faith is perfected when we see Jesus face-to-face, there will always be unfulfilled desires that we must surrender to His grace and mercy. Quite plainly, we will want things in this life that we just won't get.

I've experienced this firsthand on numerous occasions, but the greatest of these has been in my desire to raise a large family. My aunt raised me when my mother died, and for ten years it was just her and me. She was a tremendous blessing to me, but I sometimes longed for the laughter, hugs, and busy family dinners I had witnessed in the homes of friends with multiple siblings. As I got older, I dreamed of having at least four children naturally and planned to adopt more. In my mind, the larger the family, the better.

But this was not God's will for my life. My medical condition means that giving birth to children poses a life-threatening risk, while adoption poses an ethical dilemma because of the shortened life expectancy associated with Vascular Ehlers-Danlos Syndrome. I gave birth to my only son before I became aware that I have this condition, and I am incredibly blessed to have him today; but my heart will always desire more children. I have to constantly surrender this desire to God's will.

Do you have an unfulfilled desire that you aren't sure will come to fruition? If so, describe it below:

I recognize now that God's decision to withhold my desire for a large family is also an act of His mighty protection and provision. Given my medical condition, mothering a large family probably wouldn't be in my best interest for many reasons. God always knows and works for our greater good, and we have to trust that whether we understand it or not. But more important, the will of God always works for the good of His entire kingdom. Perhaps if God allowed me to have a large family, I wouldn't be able to accomplish the kingdom tasks He has set aside for me. In any case, our willingness to surrender our desires plays a part in God's effort to change the world. When we put God's will over our own desires, the world around us is changed for the good of His kingdom.

> When we put God's will over our own desires, the world around us is changed for the good of His kingdom.

Is God asking you to move forward with something today that you don't want to do? Does moving forward in His will mean that you will have to sacrifice one of your desires? If so, take heart that Jesus understands how you feel. And He can give you the strength to move forward, anyway.

Seek Him now in solace and in prayer. And when it's time to rise, do it knowing you have the strength of heaven at your side.

DAY 4: THE POWER
OF THE BREATH

"It's time," she says. The soon-to-be mother carefully makes her way to the passenger seat of the car. "Breathe in, breathe out," she tells herself. Her husband rushes the car toward the hospital, ready to see new life in the flesh. Several hours and pushes and prayers later, the tiny newborn takes her first breath in the world as we know it. Mom and Dad may not realize it, but baby's first intake of air will be one of the strongest breaths she will ever take.

What is heard in the delivery room as a cry of shock is heard in heaven as a cry of blessing. In both places, it is a cry of life. God gives life. God gives breath. They are one and the same. Baby instinctively knows she only has to receive one to have the other.

She grows older. She even forgets that the Creator of the universe sustains her life with His very breath. The world tells her that she has to work for it. The world twists the truth until she believes that she does not matter. But the world doesn't know that she cannot flee from what surrounds her—or that the lover of her soul pursues her relentlessly.

He whispers. She bends her ear toward His voice. And she turns the pages of hope to find that He has been there all along. From her first breath to her last, He is sustaining her every need. Her first breath was of His love and her last will be into His arms.

So she breathes deeply again and again. And with every breath she repeats these words: *my life matters*. Because now she remembers: Her life was not an accident, and her future is not held by chance.

Today we will consider the power of the breath.

Read Luke 23:44-56, and put a placeholder there for future reference.

The Quick Three
What happened?
Where did it happen?
What characters are mentioned in this reading?

Setting the Scene

The arrest was made. The trials came and went. The conviction was laid down. And now the time for the cross has come. Jesus has met His divine appointment in Jerusalem.

If you are like me, this passage requires many deep breaths to get through it. I cannot even read the twenty-third chapter of Luke without weeping for my King. So, inhale deeply before we dive in.

It took six days for God to create the world. It would take six hours for Jesus to bring salvation for all of humanity. Jesus was crucified around 9:00 a.m. and stayed on the cross until 3:00 p.m. Fulfilling the prophecy from Amos 8:9-10 (in the margin), darkness covered the land for three hours, which would have begun at noon.[1]

Luke does not give specific information as to the physical details of Jesus' crucifixion. The reader is left to hold the simple retelling of His death within the universal implications of His life. This is an ideal perspective for our lesson today because we are going back to the basics of life. And life, after all, is the driving focus of our study.

His Breath Within Me

Finding abundant life through intentional living has been the goal of our study of Luke. With that in mind, how are you doing?

Over the past six weeks, how have you embraced intentional, abundant life?

In what ways has your attitude toward this pursuit changed as we have studied the life of Jesus?

We're going to look at a few details in today's passage and then settle in on one key detail that might help you embrace abundant life a little more.

First, let's review the layout of the Temple in Jerusalem, which we studied in Week 1. The Temple was a permanent place of worship following the model of the Tabernacle that traveled with God's people in the wilderness:

²*A tabernacle was set up. In its first room were the lampstand and the table with its consecrated bread; this was called the Holy Place. ³Behind the second curtain was a room called the Most Holy Place, ⁴which had the golden altar of incense and the gold-*

---

⁹*"In that day," declares the Sovereign LORD,*

*"I will make the sun go down at noon
   and darken the
   earth in broad
   daylight.*
¹⁰*I will turn your
religious festivals into
mourning
   and all your
   singing into
   weeping.
I will make all of you
wear sackcloth
   and shave your
   heads.
I will make that time
like mourning for an
only son
   and the end of it
   like a bitter day."*
                        (Amos 8:9-10)

covered ark of the covenant. This ark contained the gold jar of manna, Aaron's staff that had budded, and the stone tablets of the covenant.

(Hebrews 9:2-4)

These same elements were included in the Temple (refer to the diagram on page 13). Deep inside the Temple gates was the Holy Place, which held an inner porch, the lampstead, the table of consecrated bread or shewbread, and the altar of incense (as well as the priests' rooms and storage). And within the Holy Place was the Holy of Holies, also known as the Most Holy Place.

Read Exodus 26:33. What separated the Holy Place from the Most Holy Place?

One source explains that the Most Holy Place was "inhabited only by God, and where no mortal could enter except the high priest once a year."[2] Since the formation of the Israelite nation, and with only the exception of God's direct revelation through His prophets and chosen spokespersons, the Israelites had direct access to God through the high priest alone, who would step into God's presence beyond the veil of the Temple.

What happens in Luke 23:45?

What is the significance of the veil being torn in two? What are some possible implications?

I like how Warren Wiersbe explains the miracle of the torn veil:

This miracle announced to the priests and people that the way into God's presence was open for all who would come to Him by faith though Jesus Christ (Hebrews 9:1–10:25). No more do sinners need earthly temples, altars, sacrifices, or priests, for all had now been fulfilled in the finished work of the Son of God.[3]

What does Hebrews 6:19-20 tell us about the role of Jesus for all people?

Praise the Lord that we have direct access to our heavenly Father at any time through the saving life of Jesus! All that is required is a willing heart and an earnest prayer. Is there something you have wanted to talk to God about but have wondered if He would hear or respond? Take a moment to pour your heart out to Him now; His beloved Son made it possible for the curtain to be torn in two for you so that you may approach the throne of grace with confidence (Hebrews 4:16).

In order to become our personal high priest, however, Jesus would have to sacrifice everything.

Read Luke 23:46 in the margin, and underline the words indicating that Jesus has died.

He *breathed* His *last*. With His last words, Jesus quoted Psalm 31:5, written by David. It's a verse that may have been recited often at the evening offering at the Temple, which would have taken place at around the same time as Jesus' death.[4] His last breath was an offering to His Father on behalf of the entire world.

What does each Scripture tell us about the breath of God?

Genesis 2:7

Job 33:4

Psalm 104:29-30

Isaiah 42:5

Ezekiel 37:5-6

Jesus called out with a loud voice, "Father, into your hands I commit my spirit." When he had said this, he breathed his last.

(Luke 23:46)

It is God's breath that fills and sustains us. We cannot run from it, nor do we have to work for it. We simply have to receive it. God fills us with life and love with every breath we take.

What's more, the very cessation of Jesus' breath was necessary for us to receive the gift of eternal life. His death was a holy sin offering sent to the Father so that we might live forever with God in heaven. Praise be to our wonderful Savior who gave His very breath for us! Yes, take that deep breath in right now. Every ounce of it is full of mercy, grace, and love. It's also full of life.

The Divine Benefactor

You may have read these now-famous words often attributed to Alice Morse Earle: "Yesterday is history. Tomorrow is a mystery. Today is a gift. That's why it is called the present."[5] I've seen shortened variations of this saying everywhere, including a sign that hangs in a beach house where I often stay. I've visited

Extra Insight

For a more detailed account of Jesus' death, see the Gospels of Matthew and John.

coastal North Carolina waters every summer since I was born. And every time I return I now wonder, *Will this summer be my last?* It's a morbid thought, I know. But thinking about it in light of what Jesus has done for us shifts my perspective from morbid to majestic.

Last moments are always on my mind. Last chances. Is this the last time I'll hug my son, kiss my husband, breathe in saltwater air . . . breathe in at all? Life is so precious. I want to soak it up. As it turns out, living like every moment might be my last feels like I'm living in abundance instead. Each breath holds a rare moment of blessing that repeats itself every time we are willing to acknowledge its divine benefactor.

Like walking into a dark room and turning on the light, once we realize the incalculable value of the breath of God combined with Jesus' sacrifice on the cross, it changes us. The day we recognize life as a precious gift from our heavenly Father is the day we truly start to live.

Intentionally living like Jesus means that nothing is wasted and everything is precious. And all of it points to the glory of God, because we recognize Him as the source of all life. Open your eyes to what this day holds for you. Shift your perspective from one of burden to one of blessing. Every mundane task before you is a miracle.

The day we recognize life as a precious gift from our heavenly Father is the day we truly start to live.

Spend a few minutes writing a prayer of thanks to God for the precious gift of life:

Now take a deep breath and put two feet on the floor. It's time to start living!

DAY 5: WITNESS TO LIFE

> **The thief comes only to steal and kill and destroy; I have come that they may have life, and have it to the full.**
> **(John 10:10)**

I was shocked at what greeted me as I turned out of my neighborhood one day. Where acres of lush, dense pine trees had stood the day before, I now watched construction equipment moving the remnants of tall pines from one side of a clearing to another. An energy substation was to be built, so the beautiful trees had to be cut down.

I was sad watching those trees come down, knowing that the life that had buzzed from God's creation across the street was suddenly gone.

As I went about my errands for the day, the image of those fallen trees stayed with me. I wondered how many times I had watched the very same thing happen with my friends and family. Had I been a witness to life, only to watch it fade and fall before me?

I thought of a friend who struggled with her faith after her mother died. I could have spent more time with her, but I deemed myself too busy. Or the coworker I watched make one poor choice after another. She was clearly suffering and searching for truth, yet I did little except to pray for her from afar.

Prayer is, indeed, powerful, but so are my actions when they are emulating the life of Christ. If I can be so easily convicted by watching trees die, why can't I be even more convicted watching those around me suffer when there might be something I can do to point them to Jesus?

Today we will be reminded of the glorious news that Jesus is *alive*. It's this truth that will help us encourage others onward to determined living.

Read Luke 24:1-12, and put a placeholder there for future reference.

The Quick Three
What happened?
Where did it happen?
What characters are mentioned in this reading?

Setting the Scene

This is a moment that calls for great rejoicing! The stone has been rolled away and the tomb found empty. He is risen! He is risen indeed! We began our study by instilling the habits of *worship*, *word*, *pray*, and *obey* in our everyday lives. And today, of all days, calls for us to begin with immense praise!

If you have confetti lying around in your junk drawer, throw it. If you've got balloons shoved into your closet, blow them up. Put this book down for a moment and get on your feet. Crank your praise music up loud and worship the risen Savior!

The stone being rolled away was no insignificant feat. As one source explains, "To gain access, several strong men used levers to roll the massive disk away from the opening and then wedge it into place"[1] It was highly unlikely that this had been accomplished by obscure visitors so early in the morning. Scripture doesn't tell us how the stone was moved; we are simply left to assume it was part of the wonderful miracle of Christ's resurrection.

Luke will refer to the men in "dazzling apparel" as angels later in Luke 24:23. Heavenly assistance was needed to help these women recognize the work of the risen Savior. They would need to remember it clearly because Jesus had important work for these women of the faith. Today we will consider what they witnessed at the tomb and throughout Jesus' earthly ministry. Then we'll apply that to our ultimate goal of determined living.

Let's dive in together one last time!

The Witness of a Woman

Women played a significant role throughout Jesus' ministry, and that continues to be true after his death as well.

Glance back at Luke 23:55. To whom, specifically, is Luke referring in the opening verses of chapter 24?

These are likely the same women mentioned in Luke 8:1-3. These women have followed Jesus through His entire ministry. They have been a witness to a divine life, yet they are still "perplexed" at the empty tomb.

What does the angel remind them of in Luke 24:6-8?

The women have witnessed the fact that Jesus knows death is on its way. They have witnessed His determination to travel to the cross in Jerusalem out of love for us and obedience to His Father. They are now the first witnesses to the miracle of His resurrection.

Consider all that these women have seen over the three years of Jesus' ministry. What stories do you think have stayed with them the most?

What about Jesus do you think they would be most eager to share with their friends and family?

What about you? What have you witnessed? Have you learned anything about Jesus that you didn't know before? If so, what?

Now, flip back through your book to review the themes we have studied together, and put a star by the lessons that have resonated most with you.

	Theme Review	
Week 1 The Son: Determined to Choose Life	A worshipful heart prepares us for what we may meet in the coming day.	
	By prioritizing the pursuit of wisdom, we take the first step toward accomplishing God's will for our lives.	
	A commitment to prayer increases intimacy with our heavenly Father.	
	We overcome the enemy's attempts to separate us from God when we determine to obey God's will.	
	We will fulfill our purpose on earth when we routinely display patterns of determined faithfulness.	
Week 2 The Teacher: Determined to Demonstrate a New Way	As it was with Jesus, our fruitfulness is determined by our willingness to seek spiritual rest and renewal with God.	
	God intends for the real work of His kingdom to be done in the collective.	
	A key indicator of how well we are emulating Jesus is the amount of time we spend pursuing and serving those who do not know Him.	
	Those who embrace Jesus' upside-down kingdom are radically productive toward building the kingdom of God.	
	Responding to hostility with love will help us embrace Jesus' selfless posture.	
Week 3 The Rescuer: Determined to Save Humankind	By acting with compassion toward those around us, we can help the world recognize God's tender love for humanity.	
	A grateful heart produces true devotion to the One who forgives our sins.	
	Following the divine Chain-Breaker empowers us to be lasting legacy-makers.	
	When we determine to believe Jesus, rather than just believe in Him, we'll develop a close and personal relationship with Him.	
	As followers of Jesus, we are called to recognize and restore the unmet needs of others.	

Week 4 The Healer: Determined to Love the World	To embrace our future with Christ, we must be willing to let Him heal our past.	
	The only way to fully live is to release your expectations for life and instead wait expectantly for Jesus to satisfy.	
	Determining to live like Jesus will transform us into messengers of hope in a dark and broken world.	
	Wholehearted devotion to God prompts us to leave our comfort zones to love our neighbors.	
	When our hearts are fully connected to Jesus, we are better equipped to serve others.	
Week 5 The Friend: Determined to Persevere	Embracing an eternal perspective over temporal satisfaction will make us ready to live life to the fullest.	
	Realigning our priorities with God's priorities reduces our anxiety.	
	When our hearts are broken for humanity, our commitment to living like Jesus is more steadfast.	
	God's loving determination to rescue unbelievers everywhere motivates us to welcome the repentant heart with open arms.	
	Humbly admitting our total dependence on God opens our eyes to the most vulnerable among us.	
Week 6 The Victor: Determined to Live with Courage	As determined living takes us into situations that seem hopeless, we can find courage in a God who does the impossible.	
	When we cling to Jesus, we can boldly confront difficult situations with wisdom and grace.	
	When we put God's will over our own desires, the world around us is changed for the good of His kingdom.	
	The day we recognize life as a precious gift from the heavenly Father is the day we truly start to live.	
	One of our primary jobs as believers is to serve as witnesses to Jesus' life and teachings.	

In Luke 24:9, how do the women respond to the news of Jesus' resurrection and the remembrance of His words?

With whom do they share the good news?

Because Jesus chose to appear to women first after His resurrection, R. T. France observes that as a "divine challenge to human prejudice" we should consider that Jesus holds a woman's ability to share authentic testimony with the world in high regard. He also notes that their witness brings added validity to Jesus' resurrection because it would have been highly unlikely for a Jewish person to fabricate a woman's testimony.[2] Don't miss the fact that *these women were the first post-resurrection evangelists*. If this is a challenge to human prejudice, we ought to also receive it as a challenge to us. These first-century women witnesses are passing the baton to you and me!

Time to Get to Work

What will we do with the knowledge of this precious gift? Will we hide it in our hearts and do nothing to share it with those around us? Or will we take time to share the good news of what we know about Jesus with those who need it? The efforts we have made in studying Luke's Gospel don't end here. One of our primary jobs as believers is to serve as witnesses to Jesus' life and teachings. We now have work to do.

This world needs Jesus. How can we share His love today? We can start by paying attention to the truths we have learned and then act upon them. A witness's truth should never be withheld when it can bring good to the kingdom of God.

Glance back at the chart of themes from our study. You've placed a star by the ones that resonated deeply with you. Now read through them again with your friends, family, and acquaintances in mind. Who in your circle of influence would benefit from embracing these truths?

If, as you read through the chart again, the Holy Spirit brings someone specific to mind, write his or her name next to that particular theme. Spend some time praying over the names, asking God to open doors and provide opportunities for you to share that message (and perhaps its accompanying Scripture) in some way with them, remembering that actions speak louder than words. We will be heard only when we have led with kindness, compassion, and grace.

Above all, we must remember the hope of the Resurrection so that we can determine to live like Jesus in every moment and reveal that same hope to others. This is the way to a determined, abundant life.

Before we close this day and our study, take a moment to write a prayer to Jesus. Make it a determined statement, committing to living like Him in specific ways. How will you make a difference in the kingdom of God today, sister? I know Jesus will use you in a mighty way, because I know that you will remain... determined.

> One of our primary jobs as believers is to serve as witnesses to Jesus' life and teachings. We now have work to do.

Today is also a moment worth celebrating because you have been determined to complete this study! I am so proud of you! It has been a deep privilege to walk through God's Word with you, and I pray that God has rewarded you greatly in your commitment to study the Scriptures.

So, are you determined? Are you ready to follow Jesus' example and walk out unwavering joy-filled faith every day, relying on the power of the Holy Spirit? Have you released the things that are keeping you from abundant living—or are you committed to continue working on that? Have you embraced—or will you seek to embrace—the patterns of faith that will help you live like Jesus? This is our calling, as we read in 1 Peter: "To this you were called, because Christ suffered for you, leaving you an example, that you should follow in his steps" (2:21).

As you close the pages of this study, I hope you can answer yes to every one of those questions. Most important, I hope you have intimately connected with a Savior who remains laser-focused in His mission to love you and the world around you. He is the true prize to living with determination.

When distractions come, and they will, threatening to knock you off course of living like Jesus, you can return to the pages of Luke to remind you of the truths we learned together there. God is scanning the globe for determined disciples of Jesus. Let's be ready to answer the call!

[12]*Not that I have already obtained all this, or have already arrived at my goal, but I press on to take hold of that for which Christ Jesus took hold of me.* [13]*Brothers and sisters, I do not consider myself yet to have taken hold of it. But one thing I do: Forgetting what is behind and straining toward what is ahead,* [14]*I press on toward the goal to win the prize for which God has called me heavenward in Christ Jesus.*

(Philippians 3:12-14)

Luke 24:50-53

The ascension marks the end of Jesus' earthly ministry, but it points to the

_____ of His _____.

The hope of Jesus' completed earthly mission, and His determination to see it through, bring us great _____.

The ongoing work of Jesus' ministry _____ today with you and me.

VIDEO VIEWER GUIDE ANSWERS

Week 1

choose life

wandering aimlessly

choices

Week 2

hearts

truth

know

Week 3

asleep

in control

faith / fears

Week 4

rescue

endurance

sacrifice / blessing

Week 5

need

honor

ignore / abandon

Week 6

hope / return

joy

continues

NOTES

Week 1

Day 1

1. Geoffrey Wigoder et al. *Illustrated Dictionary & Concordance of the Bible* (New York, NY: Reader's Digest Association, Inc., 1992), 978.
2. Warren W. Wiersbe, *Be Compassionate: Let the World Know That Jesus Cares: NT Commentary: Luke 1–13* (Colorado Springs, CO: David C. Cook, 2010), 36.
3. Ibid.
4. R. T. France, *Luke*. Edited by Mark L. Strauss et al. (Grand Rapids, MI: Baker Books, 2013), 40.
5. Wiersbe, *Be Compassionate*, 40.

Day 2

1. Walter A. Elwell, editor. *Baker's Evangelical Dictionary of Biblical Theology* (Grand Rapids, MI: Baker Books, 1998), https://www.biblestudytools.com/dictionary/crown/, accessed July 12, 2018.
2. Ibid.
3. Charles R. Swindoll, *Insights on Luke: Swindoll's Living Insights New Testament Commentary* (Carol Stream, IL: Tyndale House Publishers, Inc., 2017), 83.
4. Wiersbe, *Be Compassionate*, 41.
5. France, 45.
6. Wigoder et al. 183.

Day 3

1. Facts in the chart are from *Chronological Life Application Study Bible: New Living Translation* (Carol Stream, IL: Tyndale House, 2012), 1254-55, 1290; and Wigoder et al. 639, 785.
2. John MacArthur, *The MacArthur Study Bible*, "Concordance" (Nashville, TN: Thomas Nelson, Inc., 2006), 113.
3. *Chronological Life Application Study Bible*, 1254-1256.
4. Swindoll, 93-94, 97-98.
5. Ibid., 93.
6. France, 57.
7. Wiersbe, *Be Compassionate*, 45.

Day 4

1. Swindoll, 106.
2. Ibid., 104.
3. France, 66.

Day 5

1. France, 72.
2. Wiersbe, 54.
3. Swindoll, 114.
4. Craig S. Keener, *The IVP Bible Background Commentary: New Testament* (Downers Grove, IL: InterVarsity Press, 2003), 199.
5. France, 69-70.
6. Wiersbe, *Be Compassionate*, 54.
7. France, 71.
8. Swindoll, 118.
9. Ibid.

Week 2

Introduction

1. Swindoll, 122.

Day 1

1. Carl G. Rasmussen, *Zondervan Essential Atlas of the Bible* (Grand Rapids, MI: Zondervan, 2013), 115.
2. Ibid., 115-116.
3. France, 76.
4. Ibid., 78.

Day 2

1. Keener, 201.
2. Alan Thompson. *Luke: Exegetical Guide to the Greek New Testament* (Nashville, TN: Broadman & Holman, 2017), 84.
3. "Book of Acts," Got Questions, https://www.gotquestions.org/Book-of-Acts.html, accessed December 15, 2018.
4. Swindoll, 134.
5. France, 82.

Day 3

1. France, 97.
2. Swindoll, 147-148.
3. *Chronological Life Application Study Bible: New Living Translation* (Carol Stream, IL: Tyndale House, 2012), 1288.
4. Keener, 201.

Day 4

1. Swindoll, 168.
2. Thompson, 103.
3. Wiersbe, *Be Compassionate*, 78.
4. France, 113.
5. Wiersbe, *Be Compassionate*, 78.

Day 5

1. Bible Hub, s.v. "echthros,", https://biblehub.com/greek/2190.htm, accessed December 15, 2018.

2. Swindoll, 172.
3. Ibid., 173.
4. France, 113.
5. Swindoll, 172

Week 3

Day 1

1. Swindoll, 184.
2. Ibid., 186.
3. Ibid.
4. Keener, 207.
5. Wiersbe, *Be Compassionate*, 92.

Day 2

1. Swindoll, 203.
2. France, 135.
3. Swindoll, 204.
4. Wiersbe, *Be Compassionate*, 96.
5. France, 135.
6. Swindoll, 203.
7. Wiersbe, *Be Compassionate*, 98.
8. Swindoll, 203.
9. *Chronological Life Application Study Bible,*1340.

Day 3

1. France, 1-7.
2. Ibid., 6.
3. Ibid., 146-147.
4. Ibid., 148.
5. Keener, 201.
6. Anxiety and Depression Association of America, "Understanding the Facts of Anxiety Disorders and Depression Is the First Step," https://adaa.org/understanding-anxiety, accessed December 15, 2018.

Day 4

1. France, 158.
2. Wiersbe, *Be Compassionate*, 112.
3. France, 158.
4. Swindoll, 233.
5. Keener, 141.
6. Swindoll, 234.
7. France, 158, 159.
8. Ibid., 159.

Day 5

1. Corrie ten Boom, quoted in Wiersbe, *Be Compassionate*, 121.
2. France, 160.
3. Keener, 144.

Introduction

1. Winston Churchill, "Never give in, never, never, never, 1941," https://www
.nationalchurchillmuseum.org/never-give-in-never-never-never.html, accessed December 18,
2018.
2. Ibid.

Day 1

1. Swindoll, 251.
2. Wiersbe, *Be Compassionate*, 121.
3. Ibid., 45.
4. Ibid., 40.
5. France, 165.
6. Wiersbe, *Be Compassionate*, 121.
7. *Chronological Life Application Study Bible*, 36-37.
8. "Holy and Anointed One," *Word to Worship*, wordtoworship.com/song/3222, accessed
December 20, 2018.

Day 2

1. Raechel Myers and Amanda Bible Williams. *She Reads Truth: Holding Tight to Permanent in a World
That's Passing Away* (Nashville, TN: B & H Publishing Group, 2016), 2.
2. France, 165.
3. Ibid.
4. Swindoll, 253.
5. C. S. Lewis, *Till We Have Faces: A Myth Retold* (Grand Rapids, MI: Eerdmans, 1972), 267, 308.

Day 3

1. Swindoll, 277.
2. Ibid.
3. Ibid.
4. Commentary for Luke 9:51, https://www.revisedenglishversion.com/Luke/chapter9/51,
Accessed December 18, 2018.
5. "Flint Definition and Meaning—Easton's Bible Dictionary." Bible Study Tools, Salem Web
Network, www.biblestudytools.com/dictionary/flint/, accessed December 18, 2018.
6. Swindoll, 277.
7. "Flint Definition and Meaning—Bible Dictionary." Bible Study Tools, Salem Web Network,
www.biblestudytools.com/dictionary/flint/, accessed December 18, 2018.

Day 4

1. France, 188-189.
2. Swindoll, 279.
3. France, 189.
4. Ibid., 191.
5. Swindoll, 303.
6. Preemptive Love Coalition core values statement, https://preemptivelove.org/core-values/,
accessed December 18, 2018

Day 5

1. France, 195.
2. Jill Savage. "First Things First," Writer Track Meeting, She Speaks Conference, July 22, 2016, Concord, NC.
3. Swindoll, 308.

Week 5

Introduction

1. John Chambers. "Jonny Brownlee Helped over Line by Brother Alistair," YouTube, September 19 2016, www.youtube.com/watch?v=liCRrheKIOI, accessed December 21, 2018.

Day 1

1. Carol Kuruvilla. "A Pediatrician Shares Life's Meaning from His Talks with Dying Kids," *The Huffington Post*, February 3, 2018, www.huffingtonpost.com/entry/pediatrician-dying-kids -meaning-of-life_us_5a74d43ae4b0905433b41616, accessed December 18, 2018.
2. France, 212.
3. Keener, 223.
4. Wiersbe, Be *Compassionate*, 163.

Day 2

1. Habib Yaribeygi et al. "The Impact of Stress on Body Function: A Review". *EXCLI* Journal, U.S. National Library of Medicine, 2017, www.ncbi.nlm.nih.gov/pmc/articles/PMC5579396/, accessed December 18, 2018.
2. Swindoll, 361.
3. Wiersbe, Be *Compassionate*, 165.
4. Dictionary.com, s.v. "priority," www.dictionary.com/browse/priority, accessed December 18, 2018.
5. Swindoll, 363.
6. "His Eye Is on the Sparrow," words by Civilla D. Martin, music by Charles H. Gabriel, https:// library.timelesstruths.org/music/His_Eye_Is_on_the_Sparrow/, accessed December 18, 2018.
7. France, 218.

Day 3

1. "Katie Couric, NBC's Today Show Host, Lost Her…" *Sermon Central*, June 18, 2007, www .sermoncentral.com/sermon-illustrations/61322/easter-resurrection-by-sermoncentral ?ref=TextIllustrationSerps. Originally appeared in "Whatever Katie Wants," by Cable Neuhaus, in *AARP The Magazine* (US), 48, no. 6C, November 2005,44-49.
2. France, 238.
3. MacArthur, 1117.
4. France, 239.

Day 4

1. Philip Yancey. *What's So Amazing About Grace?* (Grand Rapids, MI: Zondervan, 1997), 71.
2. Keener, 232.
3. Ibid., 233.
4. Ibid.

5. Warren W. Wiersbe. *Be Courageous: Take Heart from Christ's Example: Luke 14–24* (Colorado Springs, CO: David C. Cook, 2010), 42.

Day 5

1. Keener, 239.
2. Alfred Edersheim. *The Life and Times of Jesus the Messiah: New Updated Edition* (Peabody, MA: Hendrickson, 2009), 677.
3. Keener, 239.
4. Swindoll, 471.
5. Ibid.

Week 6

Day 1

1. Wiersbe, *Be Courageous*, 92.
2. Ibid., 93.
3. France, 309.
4. William Barclay, *The Gospel of Luke*, rev. ed., Daily Study Bible (Philadelphia, PA: Westminster, 1973), 239; quoted in ibid., 312, 397.

Day 2

1. France, 314.
2. Ibid., 165.
3. Keener, 243.
4. Wiersbe, *Be Courageous*,100.
5. Swindoll, 510.

Day 3

1. Keener, 250.
2. Ibid., 251.
3. Ibid., 163.
4. Strong's Concordance, s.v. *Agónia*, https://biblehub.com/greek/74.htm, accessed December 19, 2018.
5. Wiersbe, *Be Courageous*, 139.

Day 4

1. Wiersbe, *Be Courageous*, 155.
2. Keener, 255.
3. Wiersbe, *Be Courageous*, 158.
4. Keener, 255.
5. Tian Dayton. *One Foot in Front of the Other: Daily Affirmations for Recovery* (Deerfield Beach, FL: Health Communications, Inc., 2013), 136.

Day 5

1. Swindoll, 574.
2. France, 374.